A MASTER TEACHER POSITION YOU DESERVE

A Complete Guide in Preparing Your Documents for Promotion

Elmer Z. Ventura, MA.Ed.

Published by Poetry Planet Publishing House
Rosario, Pozorrubio, Pangasinan, Philippines
Contact Number: 09554960044
Edited by Marie Ezekiel
Designed by Tess Ritumalta
Cover designed by Elmer Ventura

ISBN
978-621-8253-56-8 (hardbound)
978-621-8253-57-5 (softbound)
978-621-8253-58-2 (mobile/kindle)

Pictures used are taken in freepics.com and may contain its own copyrights

FOREWORD

It is the dream of any individual teacher to be promoted to his/her position immediately. Promotion is both a sign of being successful and active in the area of work. Promotion is also an improvement in a job that would increase pay.

Promotion is for everyone, particularly for those eager to be promoted or working hard, even if they are already in the teaching profession. Hard work, discipline, dedication, integrity, and prayer are instruments with which any successful teacher can be promoted to Master Teacher I.

This book will teach you how to prepare documents for you to get promoted quickly in DepEd.

This book on A Master Teacher Position You Deserve is aligned with the MEC Order No. 10, s. 1979 known as the IMPLEMENTING RULES AND REGULATIONS FOR THE SYSTEM OF CAREER PROGRESSION FOR PUBLIC SCHOOL TEACHERS. This book is dotted with sample proposals that serve as guideposts in the preparation of documents.

ACKNOWLEDGEMENT

This book could not have been done without the generous assistance of my family and friends, who consistently supported, devoid of any material or compensation.

For just a smile and a warm embrace, they were both ready and eager to help come rain or come shine. No amount of money or gold glitter would be enough to repay their support and motivation. Thank you so much for that.

The only reward that I can afford is my most heartfelt and true unconditional love and respect, which will always be enshrined in my heart, mind, and soul as long as I live.

Elmer Z. Ventura

PREFACE

Unsung heroes. Teachers always keeping up as education evolves to modernization and helping young minds achieve their dreams in a globally competitive environment. They pioneer ways to inculcate home-based education during this challenging era of the pandemic. Exerting themselves vigorously to enrich the lives of children, their parents, guardians, and their family despite the distance and communication limitations of communications. Yes, they are the teachers…standing behind the curtain stage while many other heroes finally emerge after their mentoring, training, and of course, their unparalleled dedication and hard work.

The author of this book, a head teacher himself, Mr. Elmer Ventura, unselfishly opened doors of opportunities for our dear heroes- our dear Teachers, for them to recognize their potentials. To see the brighter light clearly, he assists them as they trek a path leading to privileges and accomplishments they truly deserve.

He has prepared this book for achievers through revelations, instructions, and hope. As we read and study this written work, be inspired, yes be moved, as we walk along with the Author's hand guiding our directions to higher steps of success.

The Editor

CONTENTS

IMPLEMENTING RULES AND GUIDELINES ON THE SYSTEM OF CAREER PROGRESSION FOR PUBLIC SCHOOL TEACHERS BASED ON MEC ORDER NO. 10, S. 1979

Basic Policies

1. Master Teachers are instructional leaders in their respective schools/districts/divisions. They are expected to assist other teachers in the school or district/division toward improving teaching competencies and skills. They take leadership in the preparation of instructional and other materials used in the classroom. Master Teachers are also required to serve as demonstration teachers or teacher consultants in other schools within the district/division. (DepEd Order No. 7, s.2002).

2. The number of Master Teacher positions for the elementary level shall be allotted using the following formula: (MEC Order No. 1, s. 1985)

   Master Teacher I = 0.66 x number of teachers

   Master Teacher II = 0.33 x number of teachers
   Any fraction is considered one (1)

3. For the secondary level, an allotment of at least one (1) Master Teacher position per subject area with at least five (5) to seven (7) teachers shall be the basis for creating the Master Teacher position as per DECS Order No. 70, 2. 1998.

4. Positions for Master Teacher shall be allotted by division proportionally on the basis of the number of teachers. The number of positions for the division shall likewise be distributed proportionally among the districts/schools (based on MEC Order No. 10, s. 1979).

5. Only those who are actually teaching shall be considered for promotion to a Master Teacher

position. This includes teachers who, besides providing special services have regular teaching loads. (MEC Order No. 29, s. 1979).

6. Master Teachers shall be selected on the basis of the enclosed criteria provided by MEC Order No. 10, s. 1979. It is stressed that a candidate must possess all the qualifications specified unless otherwise indicated. No substitution for the qualifications required shall be allowed.

7. To fill up existing vacancies for Master Teacher positions, all qualified candidates shall be ranked based on the above-mentioned criteria.

8. For the Secondary level, subject area specialization in the undergraduate Bachelor's Degree or Master's Degree is required.

Frequently Asked Questions (FAQs)

How do I apply in DepEd as Master Teacher I or II? What is the process of application?

- Coordinate with the Schools Division Office (SDO) in your locality
- Refer to the Memorandum or Call for Applications issued by the SDO re:
    1. Vacant position for MT
    2. Salary Grade
    3. Qualification Standards
    4. Documentary Requirements
    5. List and Timeline of Activities

6. Deadlines

- Attend orientation for applicants, if any, organized by the SDO
- Due to COVID-19, SDOs may employ alternative strategies and platforms (e.g. online) in the conduct of selection processes.
    - ✓ Publication/posting of vacancies
    - ✓ Submission/receipt of application documents
    - ✓ Document review
    - ✓ PSB deliberations

What are Qualification Standards?

The Qualification Standards (QS) are the minimum qualifications in terms of Education, Training, Experience, Eligibility, as required by the CSC.

What are the QS/minimum qualifications for the Master Teacher I & II position both in elementary and secondary?

Teachers who wish to apply for a Master Teacher position should pass a screening process conducted by a Selection Committee organized by the Schools Division Superintendent. Each candidate should possess the following criteria required for each post.

A. MASTER TEACHER I

1. Permanent Teacher for at least three (3) years based on Qualification Standard Manual of 1995 (QSM1995).

Document Needed:
*One certified photocopy of the original appointment

2. Bachelor's Degree for Teachers or equivalent as provided by the Magna Carta for Teachers plus Completion of Academic Requirements (CAR) for M.A.

   Document Needed:
   * Authenticated Copy of Transcript of Records (ToR) with a statement of graduation and/or special order for graduation if a graduate of a private school.

3. At least a Very Satisfactory performance rating for three consecutive rating periods.

   Document Needed:
   *Certified Photocopy of IPCRF for the last three years duly signed by proper authorities.

4. At least three years of experience in teaching (T1 to T3)

   Document Needed:
   *Service Record

5. At least 25 points in Leadership and Potential or has been a demonstration teacher at least in the district level for elementary and school level for secondary plus 15 points in leadership and potential.
6. Must be computer literate (use of software).

B. MASTER TEACHER II

1. Master Teacher I for at least one year based on Qualification Standard Manual of 1995 (QSM 1995).
2. Very Satisfactory performance rating for at least three rating periods.
3. Bachelor's Degree for Teachers or equivalent as provided by the Magna Carta for Teachers plus completion of a Master's Degree.
4. At least 30 points including Leadership, Potentials, and Accomplishments (LPA).
5. Has been a demonstration teacher at least on the division level for both elementary and secondary.
6. Must know how to prepare instructional materials using the computer (e.g. PowerPoint/video presentations, etc.)

A candidate must possess all the qualifications indicated to be considered for a Master Teacher position. No additional points shall be given to qualifications beyond the minimum requirements. Based on MEC

Order No. 10, s. 1979, these qualifications shall only be considered in case of a tie in points for LPA. The applicant shall also be required to have a hands-on computer test and an actual teaching demonstration before appointment to said position.

Documents Needed for Demonstration Teaching:

1. Copy of the memorandum
2. Lesson Plan duly signed by the school head and PSDS
3. Observation Form (TLOC, STAR, etc.)
4. Other proofs including pictures
5. Certification signed by proper authorities

Rates and Compensation
of Master Teachers

As of January 1, 2021 (Second Tranche)

Master Teacher 1
Salary Grade 18
43,681

Master Teacher II
Salary Grade 19
48,313

Effective January 1, 2022 (Third Tranche)

Master Teacher 1
Salary Grade 18
45,203

Master Teacher II
Salary Grade 19
49,835

Effective January 1, 2023 (Fourth Tranche)

Master Teacher 1
Salary Grade 18
45,203

Master Teacher II
Salary Grade 19
49,835

OMNIBUS CERTIFICATION OF AUTHENTICITY AND VERACITY OF DOCUMENTS

The Omnibus Certification of Authenticity and Veracity of Documents is a legal document executed by an applicant authorizing the Department of Education to verify the authenticity of his/her documents submitted for applying for a Master Teacher position or promotion.

This document is an affirmation coming from the applicant that all the submitted papers are legitimate and true. This certification is usually attached with all the pertinent documents in a legal folder.

The most important part of this certificate is a notary public legalizing it. This service is typically priced between Php100-200 at a local notary public or Municipal's Public Attorney's Office.

The next page shows a sample of the said DepEd Omnibus Certification of Authenticity and Veracity of Documents.

Republic of the Philippines
Department of Education
Region III
DIVISION OF ____________
Complete Address

OMNIBUS CERTIFICATION OF AUTHENTICITY AND VERACITY OF DOCUMENTS

I, (your complete name), of (complete address) respectfully submit the herein Folder containing the documents incidental to my application for________.

I certify that these documents are authentic, true, free from any falsehood and modification from the original, and that they are actually earned in good faith by myself.

I authorize the Personnel Selection Board/Division Selection Committee to make inquiry or investigate if needed to determine whether or not these documents are authentic or true as certified.

I also understand that in the event that any of the submitted documents will be found to be falsified or fallacious, such will cause my outright disqualification from the evaluation and, consequently, for the position.

SIGNATURE OVER PRINTED NAME
DATE

Subscribed and sworn to before me this___day of___, 2021 at______, Bulacan.

NOTARY PUBLIC

1

INNOVATION PROJECTS

Republic Act No. 9155, known as Governance of Basic Education Act of 2001, provides School-Based Management (SBM). By further devolving the governance of education to schools, empowering school heads and non-teaching personnel in expanding community participation and involvement, and making the delivery of educational service to the learners more responsive, efficient, and effective through an enhanced school planning and improvement that lays down specific interventions through initiated projects in schools.

Following the Act, all teaching and non-teaching personnel are encouraged to create/innovate school-based initiatives geared towards improving the teaching-learning process and school governance.

Innovation is a process by which we establish successful ideas to create new value. It is a term used to describe solutions to problems that represent change or departure from current practice instead of progressive improvements within the existing framework. Similarly, it is a term used to modify what existed before developing ideas, techniques, and fundamentally new beliefs.

To successfully realize innovation projects, irrespective of context or setting, a different mindset is needed. The current pandemic has pushed all learning communities to test all ideas and filter which of these ideas are practical and feasible for learning continuity. Our willingness to take risks has minimized possible learning losses in education. Innovation in teaching and learning delivery is indeed inevitable. The innovation should be interactive and innovative to respond to the needs, interests, and abilities of diverse learners

Guidelines in Conducting a Project for Innovation in School

The proposed project should be aligned with DepEd thrusts and contributory to attaining the Department's Vision and Mission. The proponent must present the reasons for the project, what needs or problems he/she wants to solve/address and innovate.

The proposed project must be qualified to benefit the learners and other school stakeholders. The proposed project must have a realistic management plan and the resources needed to complete it within a calendar year.

Sources of a fund to sustain the project must be donations, Income-Generating Project (IGP), etc. It should not be taken from the school MOOE fund. Solicitation is prohibited.

The proponent must show proof of donation, MOA, or any evidence of the project's sourcing.

When the project is already complete, the evaluators will monitor the project again and issue an evaluation form to show that it is already accomplished. The evaluation should be a requisite for the approval of the final report.

While the project is ongoing, the project evaluators will come and visit to monitor implementation status.

If the proponent will use the project proposal as "innovation" for promotion purposes, acceptance of the project depends on the PSB (Personnel Selection Board).

The project must have a provision for sustainability and replicability.

Four Types of Innovation Projects

A. Curriculum Materials or Instructional Materials

B. Original Effective and Innovative Teaching
   Techniques or Strategies

C. Simplified Work as in Reporting System,
   Records keeping, etc. or Procedures that
   Resulted to Cost Reduction

D. Worthwhile Income Generating Project (IGP)
   for Learners and given recognition from
   higher officials in the division

A
Curriculum Materials or Instructional Materials

Curriculum Materials or Instructional Materials is new, original, and self-initiated (DECS Order No. 54, s. 1993). It refers to the alternate means of communication that a classroom teacher may use to build a concept during the teaching and learning process. These include **modules, workbooks, practice sets, audio/video materials**, etc., duly approved by the Schools Division Superintendent (SDS). All innovations must be appropriately documented and duly certified by the head of office/supporting authority where it was adopted, implemented, started, and conceptualized.

Instructional material content and development and its impact after execution shall include supporting proof of data, data interpretation, and statistical validation.

Learning Modules

The module may be described as a unit, chapter, topic, or instruction fragment. It's a standard unit or an instructional portion of a lesson that's a "self-contained" piece of instruction. A week is a typical module length, but it can be shorter or longer depending on the material and the teaching style.

It must contribute to the refinement of existing and the development of new modules in line with these principles:

- interactive
- informal and conversational in style
- incorporate self-assessment
- contextualized in everyday situations
- culture-responsive/sensitive
- gender-responsive
- project-based learning
- authentic assessment
- suitable for self-learning

Parts of a Module

Title: It should be concise and descriptive of its content.

Table of contents: This part orients the learners to the Self-Learning Module (SLM).

The purpose or general aim: It provides the learner with a clear indication of the topic area covered.

Pre-requisites: This part identifies the knowledge, skills, attitudes, and experiences that the learner should pass before attempting to complete the SLM.

The instructional objective: This part is written in clear and specific behavioral terms.

Behavioral Objective: This is needed to be written in clear and specific behavioral terms. It is useful to inform the learner of the SLM's instructional intent and make explicit what is expected of the learner. It should include only a few objectives.

Direction for use: It provides a clear and concise explanation of each component in the package, what it consists of, where to find it, how to use it, and how best to proceed in completing the SLM.

Introduction: It includes a brief introduction about the topic.

Learning activities: This part includes any combination of the learning strategies: reading a set of journal articles or book chapters, viewing videotapes, using the equipment, completing written practice exercises. Some SLM may also require that learners practice specific clinical skills in a simulated or actual patient care setting.

Pretest: This part relates directly to the instructional objectives for the SLM. The pretest is using for the following purposes:

- To provide a baseline performance measure for later comparison with the post-test score.
- To indicate to the learner which sections or subsections of SLM they will need to complete and which team may be bypassed.
- To show the passing score that must be achieved so that learners will know whether they need to complete the SLM or not.

Content: It consists of small segments of information. The content is frequently separate into a different direction with questions that view, reinforce and apply to learn. The answers to this self-assessment question are provided at the end of that section of information. This part affords immediate feedback or progress and performance.

Instructional Aides: The instructional aides included in the module as readings, handouts, worksheets, written case studies, copies of policies or procedures, practice, exercises, study questions, audiovisual media, computer, bibliography suggested.

Post-test: It must cover all objectives. If it revealed that they had met goals, the student could proceed to another module. If not, the student must repeat activities to achieve what is required.

Practice Sets

It is a teacher-developed material used to reinforce the teaching and learning process intended to help a learner become proficient. Teachers locally make it to meet the specific learning resources need.

Parts of Practice Sets

1. Name of Learner, Grade Level, Section, and Date
2. Title of the Activity
3. Learning Competency with Code
4. Directions/Instructions
5. Activities

1-3 activities
(easy, average, difficult)
Procedure
Questions
6. Rubrics (if applicable)
7. Closure

Technical Specifications

Document Set-up

Paper Size:	8.27 x 11.69 inches (A4)
Margins:	1 inch all sides
Page Layout:	K-3 – Landscape
	Grade 4-12 – Portrait
Paper Quality:	80 gsm
Number of Pages:	1-3
Number of Words:	Minimal wording
Tables:	Scaffold with tables
Format:	Focus more on the content (if possible, black and white printing)

Technical Specifications for Printing

Art to Text ratio if needed:

Kinder to Grade I	65:35
Grade II	60:40
Grade III	50:50
Grade IV	40:60
Grade V-VI	30:70

Required Typeface

Grade level	Recommended Font	Font Size			Line Space	Alignment
		Text	Heads	Sub-Heads		
K-2	Century Gothic except question mark-Arial	16-pt	30-20-pt, bold	18-16 pt	4-pt	Flush (left/right)
3	Century Gothic except question mark-Arial	14-pt	28-18-pt, bold	16-14 pt	4-pt	
4	Arial/Times New Roman	14-pt	28-18-pt, bold	16-14 pt	3-pt	
5-12						

Workbook

It is a compilation of activity sheets (by unit, chapter, quarter) that will be used by the learners to practice what they are learning in a class and reinforce the lesson presented in the textbook.

It can facilitate teachers to achieve desired learning outcomes.

Front Cover Specifications

Entry	Font Type	Font Size	Other Details
Workbook Title	A serif or Sans-serif typeface with large and height, open counters, contrast, good linkage, uniform proportions	48-72 pt	Color: CMYK Mode
Resource Identifier (Workbook)	(same as the title)	18-24 pt	Position: **between the Workbook title and Cover Photo**

Grade Level Identifier (Hindu Arabic Number)	(same as the title)	50-80 pt Bold	Position: **Top Right-hand corner** Box Size: 1.5" x 1.5" Background Color: White
Violator **NOT FOR SALE HINDI IPINAGBIBILI**	(same as the title)	11 pt	Position: Rotate 20 degrees' top left-hand corner Border: Solid black: 2 lines (top and bottom) (inner light color and outside)
Cover Art/Photo	(same as the title)		Learners Material in Full Color
Name/s of Author/writer	(same as the title)	14-24 pt	Name/s of developers should be represented in a bulleted list (.)
DepEd Identifier Departmet of Education Republic of the Philippines Kagawaran ng Edukasyon Republika ng Pilipinas		15 pt Bold	Position: Bottom Center Color: Black or white depending on the background color

Color Coding of Workbook
Per Learning Area

Learning Area	Background Color for Cover
English	Cyan/Light Blue
Filipino	Dark Blue
Science	Orange
Mathematics	Green
Araling Panlipunan	Red
Edukasyon sa Pagpapakatao	Brown
Music and Arts	Canary Yellow
Physical Education and Health	Light Yellow

Mother Tongue-Based Multilingual Education (MTB-MLE)	White
Edukasyong Pantahanan at Pangkabuhayan (EPP) / Technology and Livelihood Education (TLE)	Violet

Documents Required

- ✓ Approved proposal/program of action **2pts**

- ✓ Evidences/proofs of implementation. This includes the sample of instructional materials developed, pictures, certification from superior, other proofs. **4pts**

- ✓ Impact/contributions of the project to beneficiaries. (Points to be given shall be based on the attainment of the objectives stated in the proposal. One point for every objective attained, maximum of 4 points.) **4pts**

- ✓ The project was adopted by other schools / districts / division. From ten points the following distribution scheme shall apply. If the project was adopted at the:

Elementary
a) school-level only – 2pts
b) school and district level - 4pts
c) school, district, and division level – 6pts
d) school, district, division, and regional level - 8pts
e) school, district, division, regional, and national level – 10 pts

Secondary

a) school level only – 4pts

b) school and division level – 6pts

c) school, division and regional level - 8pts

d) school, division, regional and national level – 10 pts

Sample Proposal for Innovation

January 1, 2021

Office of the Schools Division Superintendent

Sir:

I would like to request permission from your good office to develop instructional material (practice sets) in Mathematics 5 to be of help to the field specially in grade V teachers to facilitate learning with ease and enjoyment during the new normal set-up of education. This project is entitled: K TO 12 PRACTICE SETS IN MATHEMATICS 5.

Rest assured that during the development of the instructional material, no school program operation will be interrupted; and a copy of final of the material will be submitted to the Division Office. Attached here is the project proposal for your immediate reference.

Thank you and I am hoping that this request will merit your approval.

Respectfully yours,

Proponent

Noted:

Reviewed by:

____
School Head

____
EPSVr

Recommending Approval:

____
Chief Education Supervisor
Curriculum Implementation Division

APPROVED:

____
Schools Division Superintendent

PROJECT PROPOSAL

I. Project Description:

Title: K TO 12 PRACTICE SETS IN MATHEMATICS 5
Proponent: Juan Dela Cruz
Project Site: ABC Elementary School

II. Rationale:

To support DepEd's K to 12 reforms, development of instructional material is committed to be undertaken by the proponent in coordination with DepEd Tarlac Province particularly the Curriculum and Implementation Division under the guidance and technical leadership of the EPS in Mathematics.

The development of an instructional material for grade V will redound to the fulfillment of the Education for All (EFA) Goals, Millennium Development Goals (MDGs) and the Basic Education Social Reform Agenda (BESRA) and will contribute to the effective implementation of the K to 12 Program during the new normal set-up of education.

According to Hand (2000) educators specializing remediation to specific challenges on education, instructional material can help develop independent learners and critical thinkers in Mathematics. Therefore, to make mathematics easy to understand, it requires the development of instructional material that can be used to improve pupils' ability to learn mathematics efficiently in the long run.

It is in this premise that the proponent will develop practice sets as an instructional material to make pupils achieve the competencies expected.

III. General Objectives

1. To determine the least learned learning competencies of Grade V pupils in Mathematics.
2. To construct practice exercises in each learning competency that will be included in developing an instructional material.
3. Ascertain the content validity of the developed Mathematics V IM in terms of objectives, key concepts, direction/instructions, practice exercises, reflections and topics; and
4. Identify the level of acceptability of the developed IM in terms of clarity, usefulness, language and style, illustrations, presentations, and suitability.

IV. Materials

K-12 Framework
Mathematics Curriculum Guide in Grade V (MELCs-based)
Grade 5 Teachers' Guide in Mathematics
Grade 5 Learner's Material in Mathematics
Laptop
Printing Materials

V. Project Implementation Strategies

The R and D or researched-based development methodology stages will be utilized in the development of the instructional material. The following steps can explain the development process:

Step 1. Research and information collecting, planning the materials and developing the preliminary draft of the Math activities;

Step 2. Developing the preliminary draft of the instructional material;

Step 3. Validation of the instructional material by Math experts;

Step 4. Using the results of the validation for revisions. If the results are favorable in showing the effectiveness of the instructional material, then revision is not necessary;

Step 5. After the validation process and the approval by the CID, the instructional material shall be produced and distributed to the Grade V teachers in soft copies and can be published in the Division Learning Resources Management and Development System (LRMDS) portal and

Step 6. Identifying the Implications of the instructional material in teaching Mathematics.

VI. Budget Source

Self-help. The proponent will shoulder all the necessary expenses in reproducing the learning material.

Respectfully yours,

____

Proponent

Noted:

_______________________ Reviewed by:

School Head

____

EPSVr

Recommending Approval:

____

Chief Education Supervisor
Curriculum Implementation Division

APPROVED:

____

Schools Division Superintendent

26

B

Original Effective and Innovative Teaching Techniques or Strategies

This could be a developed intervention program/technique/strategy based on the outcome of the research.

Documents Required

✓ Approved proposal/program of action signed by the SDS **2pts**

✓ Evidences/proofs of implementation. (Sample Detailed Lesson Plan using the strategy/teaching technique, recorded demonstration teaching, record of formative and summative test results during the implementation period, etc.) **4pts**

✓ Impact/contributions of the project to beneficiaries. (Improved academic achievement of the pupils/students from___ to___). Points to be given shall be based on the attainment of the objectives
As stated in the proposal. One point for every objective attained, maximum of 4 points.) **4pts**

✓ Project was adopted by other schools / districts / division. **10pts**

From the ten points, the following distribution scheme shall apply. If the project was adopted at the:

Elementary

a) school-level only – 2pts

b) school and district level - 4pts

c) school, district, and division level – 6pts

d) school, district, division, and regional level - 8pts

e) school, district, division, regional, and national level – 10 pts

Secondary

a) school level only – 4pts

b) school and division level – 6pts

c) school, division, and regional level - 8pts

d) school, division, regional, and national level – 10 pts

C
Simplified Work as in Reporting System, Records keeping, etc. or Procedures that Resulted to Cost Reduction

This could be the product of a Continuous Improvement (CI) program, research findings, or the results of comparative studies.

Documents Required

✓ Approved proposal/program of action **2pts**

✓ Evidences/proofs of implementation. (Sample of the Output (e.g. forms), Pictures, Testimonies, Certifications form immediate superior. **4pts**

✓ Impact/contributions of the project to beneficiaries. (Points to be given shall be based on the attainment of the objectives stated in the proposal. One point for every objective attained, maximum of 4 points.) **4pts**

Elementary
a) school level only – 2pts
b) school and district level - 4pts
c) school, district, and division level – 6pts
d) school, district, division, and regional level - 8pts
e) school, district, division, regional, and national level – 10 pts

Secondary
a) school level only – 4pts
b) school and division level – 6pts
c) school, division, and regional level - 8pts
d) school, division, regional, and national level – 10 pts

D

Worthwhile Income Generating Project (IGP) for Learners and given recognition from higher officials in the division.

Income Generating Project is a teacher initiative that makes income to fund a school program or project operation like improving the school facilities, offering scholarships to poor children, and financing a project for innovation in school. IGP is carefully planned to generate income to achieve a particular aim or target, leading to a solution to a perceived problem. It can be in the form of small businesses conducted within the school on agriculture, livelihood, technology, industry, and services with applied new approaches and with marketing done inside and outside the school. It is not a GPTA, HRPTA, School project, or another agency-initiated project.

The IGP proposal must be submitted to the SDO for approval at least one (1) month before implementing the suggested format. Only those IGP's approved by the SDS shall be credited for promotion.

The IGP shall be for the learners. The IGP shall be recorded or in existence for at least two (2) consecutive years with a minimum net income of P20,000-30,000.00.

The terminal report shall contain how the income was generated, how much was generated, where the income was used.

Fund-raising events are not considered to be an Income-Generating Project.

Accepted Income Generating Products/Services

- Horticulture: vegetable, herbs, spices, nuts
- Plants/seedlings/condiments/pickles/peanut butter/ dried herbs
- Fruits – jam/juice/fruit wine
- Cash crops – coffee/cocoa
- Flowers
- Mushrooms
- Trees – furniture
- Facility based-services
- Eco-tourism: school shop
- Internet café
- Processing facilities
- School-managed enterprises

Tips in Conducting an IGP

1. The proposed IGP should be aligned with DepEd thrusts, and contributory to the attainment of the Department's Vision and Mission.
2. The proposed IGP must be qualified to benefit the learners and other school stakeholders.
3. The proposed IGP must have a realistic management plan and the resources needed to complete the project within two (2) school years from the date of approval.
4. Sources of a fund for the IGP should not be taken from the school MOOE fund.

5. The proponent must show proof of donation (if any), Memorandum of Agreement (MOA), or any evidence of IGP's sourcing.

6. If the proponent uses the IGP for promotion purposes, he/she must have a Certificate of Completion as proof of completion of the project. It should be noted that in the application for promotion or reclassification to Master Teacher position, the Income Generating Project (IGP) is just one of the criteria under Leadership Potential that is given credit points.

7. The IGP must have a provision on Project Risk Management due to the occurring Covid-19 Pandemic and sustainability.

8. All submitted IGP proposals and Completed Project Terminal Reports are subjected to a processing period with a minimum of fifteen (15) working days upon endorsement to the Social Mobilization and Networking Unit. This processing period will rest once the document is returned to the project proponent for compliance and endorse again at the Division Office. Moreover, proposals and reports that are non-compliant, as well as not feasible in which subject for disapproval, will endorse to the Records Unit can return to the project proponent immediately.

9. Duplication and/or plagiarism of an IGP from another proponent will be subjected to disapproval.

Documents Required

- ✓ Approved proposal/program of action **2pts**

- ✓ Evidences/proofs of implementation (pictures, video, etc.) **4pts**

- ✓ Impact/contributions of the project to beneficiaries. (Certifications, financial statement of income, testimonies)
(Points to be given shall be based on the attainment of the objectives stated in the proposal. One point for every objective attained, maximum of 4 points.) **4pts**

- ✓ Project was adopted by other schools/districts/division. **10pts**

  From the ten points, the following distribution scheme shall apply. If the project was adopted at the:

Elementary
a) school-level only – 2pts
b) school and district level - 4pts
c) school, district, and division level – 6pts
d) school, district, division and regional level - 8pts
e) school, district, division, regional and national level – 10 pts

Secondary
a) school-level only – 4pts
b) school and division level – 6pts
c) school, division and regional level - 8pts

d) school, division, regional, and national level
— 10 pts

Note: *It must develop life-long learning skills among learners and implemented continuously within two years.*

Suggested Outline for
Income Generating Project Proposal

I. Project Summary Information
    1. Project Title
    2. Proponent
    3. Address/Project Site
    4. Contact Persons
    5. Number of Beneficiaries
    6. Total Project Cost
    7. Source of Funds

II. Rationale
    It includes the following:
- School situation why the project being proposed is narrated.
- School/office baseline data of the project are presented.
- The problem and importance of the project are clearly stated.

III. Project Objectives
    A. General objective addresses the problem
    B. Specific objectives are specific, measurable, attainable, results-oriented, and time-bound

IV. Proposed IGP
    Presents the following:
- The purpose of the IGP is well defined.

- It is unique in terms of implementation and production techniques.
- There is no disruption of classes in its implementation.
- There are no money-making contests involved in its conduct.
- Participants' involvement is clear.
- Novelty in IGP that supports formative growth.
- Relevance of the IGP to learners' context.
- Description of how it will be done.

V. Source of Capital and Materials

Example:

- For production project (particular item, period, and cost)
- For equipment, supplies, and tools (particular item, description, and costs)
- For administrative expenses (particulars - monitoring and evaluation and training on financial record keeping)

VI. Strategies for Implementation

- Specific activities per stage are provided. Personnel involved, expected output, and target date are stated.

Activities (detailed Sequence)	Objectives	Resources			Time Frame
		Human	Financial	Materials	
Planning Phase					
Preparation Phase					
Implementation Phase					
Post-Implementation Phase (Evaluation & Assessment)					

Workplan of Activities

- Time frame or duration (may be divided by month/quarter) can be presented in a table or Gantt chart.

Activities	Time Frame											
	J	F	M	A	M	J	J	A	S	O	N	D
Activity 1												
Activity 2												
Activity 3												

VII.   Expected Output

- Production Capacity and expected outputs
- Projected Summary of Gross Sale of Products/Profit

VIII.   Project Risk Management

- This section details the major project risks and delineates the plans to alleviate or control them.
- Make sure to address each risk's likelihood of occurring as well as its impact on the project and the school.

Risk Identification	Causes	Impact on the Project/School	Mitigation	Contingency Plan
• Risk Description • Risk Owner				

IX.   Monitoring and Evaluation Plan

- Provides a Monitoring and Evaluation Plan indicating the:
    a) activities to be evaluated
    b) evaluators
    c) the success indicators
    d) frequency
- Must include also mechanisms on financial safekeeping of profit/income.

Activities	Evaluator/s	Target Date	Expected Output

X.   Sharing of Income

- Specify 60% share for learners involved, 40% school share.

XI.   Sustainability Plan

- Explain the potential of the project and its feasibility.
- For the project to be sustained what do you plan to do?

XII.   References

XIII.   Attachments

1. Parent consent for learners' involvement (refer to DepEd Order No. 66, s. 2017).
2. Certification from the school head/principal that the IGP is not a GPTA/HRPTA project and not a Regular Program of Deped or another agency.

Sample Evaluation Criteria of IGP Proposal

Criteria	VS	S	NS	Poor
1. RATIONALE-must indicate the following: • school situation why the project being proposed is narrated. • School/Office baseline data of the project is presented. • Problem and importance of the project is clearly stated.				
2. OBJECTIVES • General objective addresses the problem • Specific objectives are specific, measurable, attainable, results-oriented, and time-bound				
3. PROPOSED IGP – presents the following: • Purpose of the IGP is well defined. • It is unique in terms of implementation and production techniques. • There is no disruption of classes in its implementation. • There are No money-making contests involved in its conduct. • Participants' involvement is clear. • Novelty in IGP that supports formative growth. • Relevance of the IGP to learners' context. • Description of how it will be done.				
4. Strategies for Implementation • Specific activities per stage are provided. • Personnel involved, expected output, and target date are stated.				

5. MONITORING AND EVALUATION – provides a Monitoring and Evaluation Plan indicating the: • activities to be evaluated • evaluators • the success indicators • frequency				
6. SHARING OF INCOME • Specify 60% share for learners involved, 40% school share				
7. RISK MANAGEMENT				
8. SUSTAINABILITY • For the project to be sustained what do you plan to do.				
9. TOTAL (IGP Proposal)				
NOTE: Proposal must score at least 24 points out of a maximum of 32 points to pass the criterion.	**PASSED**		**FAILED**	

Sample IGP Proposal

I. Title of the Project:
Efficient Seedling Production: An Income Generating Project to Augment School Nursery Improvement and Procurement of School Supplies

II. Location of the Project:
ABC ELEMENTARY SCHOOL

III. Project Proponent

       Proponent: Juan Dela Cruz
                                 Teacher-III

       Participants: School Head
                                 All EPP Teachers
                                 Indigent pupils
                                 Volunteer Parents
                                 Job Order

       Time Frame: November 2020-December 2022

IV. Rationale:

Uninterrupted habitat denudation, loss of forests, the increased deforestation of inhabitants for the forest to farms/subdivisions, urban use, grazing land, commodity plantations, and settlements have resulted in a severe problem: global climate change.

Removal of trees without adequate reforestation has resulted in habitat destruction, biodiversity loss, and aridity. Productive agricultural areas usually incur severe adverse soil loss, often degrading to the wilderness, causing the extinction of diversified ecosystems, and now evolving climatic conditions such as drought and floods.

In response to this timely call, the proponent with the help of all EPP teachers, initiated a diversified production of large-scale seedlings to make an enormous contribution to this initiative. In its boldness to accomplish its goal, the proponent set up a nursery where the seedlings are propagated and grown to a functional scale. The nursery will be the source of the seedlings for operation: tree planting and for sale. The plants/seedlings to be reared are wood trees and fruit trees. But forest trees, particularly the mahogany species, will be the majority of the seedlings for mass production.

The primary buyers of seedlings will be multi-purpose cooperatives, barangay authorities, government, private sector, and other industries who have decided to purchase their stocks for their tree-planting projects, the promoter of mass-producing seedlings as a means of income or revenue-generating project through which seedlings can be sold to the general public.

Sample IGP Proposal

V. Objectives:

A. General

This project will be conducted to supply a massive supply of forest trees and fruit-bearing trees, for tree-planting operations, for sale, for the procurement of building materials for school nursery and sports materials.

B. Specific

- To cultivate various types of seedlings (forest trees, fruit trees) in black bags to be sold for profit.
- To train indigent pupils and parents on real soil management activities to cultivate seedlings, knowledge transfer, and optimistic features – such as resourcefulness and business.
- To demonstrate that sustainable gardens use bio-waste and other organic compounds that can be used as fertilizers, nutrients can be used for pest management purposes.

VI. Project Description:

A. Location

ABC Elementary School. The Income Generating Project will implement in the nursery and other empty areas of the campus. Indigent pupils and parents who are actively interested in developing large-scale seedlings are persons involved in the project.

B. Beneficiaries

The beneficiaries of the initiative will be the underprivileged pupils of ABC Elementary School who will grow seedlings within the school nursery. The majority of indigent students who are directly interested in the forestry project are expected to develop their natural and instilling in their minds the importance of saving mother earth and climate change consciousness, environmental protection, restoration, and recovery. They will also gain the value of resourcefulness, entrepreneurship, and harmonious working relationships with their peers.

Components of the Project

1. The pupils will take the seeds of pod trees that fall from mature trees; and the seeds from their homes. Commercial sources can also be obtained.
2. Seedling (Fruit trees & wood trees) will come from the school nursery.
3. Compost, humus soil will come from a composting pit begun last year.
4. Black bags, sprinklers, organic compounds will be supplied.

Sample IGP Proposal

5. If the stock of soil at school is drained, the community's garden soil will be obtained.

C. Mechanics and Implementation
1. Fruit crops, wood trees will be planted for additional income for the construction of a nursery school and procurement of sports facilities for athletes.
2. Organic fertilizers have to be composted and collected after 4 to 6 months.
3. The mass-produced seedlings will be sold after 3-4 months or after they have grown to a reasonable scale.

D. Manpower
1. Selected indigent pupils and parents will be organized and will be closely monitored and directly assigned to each project area (nursery garden). These indigent pupils and parents would work early in the morning and late in the afternoon to avoid interrupting classes. Parents' permissions would be sought from the indigent pupils concerned.
2. These indigent pupils will be split into committees as follows: (a) Forest trees/Fruit trees Production Committee, (b) Nursery, (c) Watering Committee, (d) Control of Pests and Diseases Committee, (e) Organic Fertilizer.

2

SUBJECT COORDINATOR / GRADE CHAIRMAN / ADVISER OF SCHOOL PUBLICATION OR ADVISER OF ANY SPECIAL SCHOOL ORGANIZATION

Your principal or school head will give you special assignments and coordinatorship, but don't worry about having them, instead, perform your duties properly. Your designations are going to help you get promoted.

A teacher who served as a subject coordinator with not less than 5 teachers or Grade Chairman of not less than 5 teachers for at least two (2) school years; or adviser of school publication or any special school organization like a dramatic club, science club, etc. and discharged such assignments satisfactorily for at least 2 years provided such assignments or services are in addition to and not considered part of the regular teaching loads shall get a maximum of 12 points in the ranking if fully documented.

The school head must sign the official designation with a reference word and annotation or assertion that such coordination/chairmanship is beyond his/her daily teaching load.

A copy of the school program shall be submitted as a supporting document.

Action Plan and Accomplishment Report duly noted/certified by the School Head corroborated by at least 5 teachers.

Subject Coordinator

The Subject Coordinator shall be responsible for the supervision and administration of the Department/

District School. The Subject Coordinator shall head a group of teachers to contribute to school learners' well-being and welfare. In their leadership, the subject Coordinator models a deep understanding of the subject and outstanding teaching experience for others. The Subject Coordinator will foster professional development experiences and meetings with the teachers and inspire their members to be the best.

Main Functions

- Ensure that all classes in the department or district schools use appropriate evidence-based methods.
- Actively promote and maintain that school-wide priority areas are integrated into departmental activities.
- Experience coaching a wide variety of yearly groups/levels within the department or district schools.
- Track student results in the department or district schools and, if possible, make reasonable changes.

Grade Chairman

A Grade Chairman assumes a wide range of roles to support at least 5 teachers and student success in a particular grade.

Main Functions

Enable their colleagues to share educational tools. This can include databases, teaching books, readings, or other services to be used by learners. They can also exchange technical services such as journals, books, DLL, and evaluation methods.

- Encourages colleagues to incorporate effective instructional methods. This could provide suggestions for differentiating teaching or preparing lessons in collaboration with fellow teachers.
- Understand the grade requirements, how the different elements of the program relate together, and how the grade-level curriculum should be incorporated in the preparation of teaching and evaluation is important to ensure effective execution of the curriculum in a particular grade.
- Facilitate initiatives for practical learning among grade-level teachers.

Documents Required

1. Claim as Subject Coordinator or Grade Chairman for at least 2 years
    - ✓ Certification for serving as a subject coordinator and satisfactorily discharged such assignments or services are in addition to and not considered part of the regular load, corroborated by at least 5 teachers and duly notarized.
    - ✓ Designation as Coordinator signed by the PSDS for District Coordinatorship and school heads for School Coordinatorship.
    - ✓ Accomplishment report signed by the PSDS for District Coordinatorship and school heads for School Coordinatorship.
    - ✓ Action Plan

School Paper Adviser

A School Paper Adviser is a selected teacher by the school administration from a list of recomendees submitted by the publication staff. In the case of school paper advisers, at least one (1) publication per year is printed or mimeographed with the applicant's name indicated as the adviser.

Qualifications

- A teacher with a degree in journalism, a bachelor's degree, a master's degree, or a specialty.
- A teacher with a bachelor's degree in English, a master's degree, or a specialty.
- A teacher with experience working in the media.
- A teacher with more than the average background in journalism or paperwork at school.
- A teacher who teaches social studies.

Main Function

He / She must find a balance between managing the work and giving students the right to create their publication that faithfully represents the student population's voice.

Documents Required

- ✓ Designation as Subject Coordinator or Grade Chairman by School Head & District Supervisor. **3pts**

✓ Class/intermediate program with teaching loads on the school year being claimed/proofs of implementation of Action Plan / Calendar of Activities (Pictures, Accomplishment report, testimonies) **3pts**

✓ Impact/contributions of the project to beneficiaries. (Points to be given shall be based on the attainment of the objectives stated in the proposal. One point for every objective attained, maximum of 6 points.) **6pts**

Adviser of Interest Clubs

✓ Designation signed by the school head and PSDS.
✓ Class/Intermediate Program with teaching loads on the SY being claimed.
✓ Action Plan approved by School Head and PSDS.

✓ 2 copies of publications for the 2 years being claimed.

Sample Designation for SPA

Designation as School Paper Adviser

To: **MR. JUAN DELA CRUZ**
      Teacher III

In the exigency of the service you are hereby designated as Adviser in School Publication at ABC Elementary School effective January 1, 2021 in addition to your regular teaching loads.

As adviser of a School Publication, you are tasked to:

- Develop/Enhance the journalistic skills of pupil/student in news writing, editorial writing, feature writing, science writing, sports writing, photojournalism, editorial cartooning, desktop and online publishing, and radio broadcasting and scriptwriting;
- Enhance pupils' skills on journalism;
- Produce quality student publications as avenues for the practice of freedom of expression and responsible journalism;
- Improve the school performance in the schools' division conference;
- Formulate annual work plans on campus journalism for SY 2021-2023.

This designation does not carry with any additional remuneration or priority of promotion.

____
School Head

____
PSDS

Conforme:

____
MR. JUAN DELA CRUZ
      Teacher III

ACTION PLAN IN CAMPUS JOURNALISM

KEY RESULT AREAS	OBJECTIVES/ TARGETS	PROJECTS/ PROGRAMS	ACTIVITIES/ STRATEGIES	TIME FRAME	SOURCE OF FUNDS	EXPECTED OUTPUTS
Teacher Development	Enhance competence and skills in campus journalism of school paper adviser	Division Training of Trainers on Campus Journalism and School Paper Management	Attend Division Training on Campus Journalism and School Paper Management	May 2021	MOOE Donation	School paper adviser has been enhanced competence and skills in campus journalism
Pupil Development	Train at least 14 pupils in campus journalism	School-Based Training in Campus Journalism	Proposal Making Preparation of Activities Training-Workshop	July 2021	PTA Donation	At least 14 pupils have been trained in campus journalism
	Win at least 4 categories at the district competition level Win at least 4 categories in municipal/division competition level	District Press Conference	Preparation for the competition Coaching and mentoring	August 2021	MOOE PTA Donation	At least 4 categories have been won at the district competition level
	Win at least 4 categories in municipal/division competition level	Municipal Press Conference	Preparation for the competition Coaching and mentoring	August 2021	MOOE PTA Donation	At least 4 categories have been won in municipal/division competition level
Student Publication	Organize the Editorial Staff of the student publication	The Pillar Student Publication	Workshop in each category	July 2021	PTA Donation	Organized editorial staff of the student publication
	Publish one issue of student publication before the end of the school year	The Pillar Student Publication	Preparation for the student publication Assigning articles to the journalists Layouting and Editing	June-August 2021	PTA Donation	At least one issue of student publication has been published before the end of the school year
	Win at least one page in the Division Press Conference	The Pillar Student Publication	Preparation for the student publication Assigning articles to the journalists	March 2021	PTA Donation	At least one page has been won in the Division Press Conference

Sample Designation for Coordinatorship

Designation as District Coordinator/Specialist in AP

To: **MR. JUAN DELA CRUZ**
  Teacher III

In the exigency of the service you are hereby designated as District Coordinator/Specialist in Araling Panlipunan at ABC District effective January 1, 2021 in addition to your regular teaching loads.

As a district coordinator, you are tasked to:

- Coordinate and monitor programs/activities related to AP;
- Formulate annual action plans in Araling Panlipunan for SY 2020-2022;
- Organize and facilitate seminars and workshops for teachers teaching AP;
- Attend scheduled meetings/trainings;
- And other duties as may be required by the District Supervisor.

This designation does not carry with any additional remuneration or priority of promotion.

____
PSDS

Conforme:

MR. JUAN DELA CRUZ
  Teacher III

ACTION PLAN IN ARALING PANLIPUNAN

KEY RESULT AREAS	PROGRAM OF PROJECT	OBJECTIVES	ACTIVITIES/ STRATEGIES	TIME FRAME	SOURCE OF FUNDS	EXPECTED OUTPUTS
Learners' Development	SPG Brigada Bayanihan	Promote leadership to the young mind leaders.	SPG involvement in Brigada Bayanihan	Feb-Mar 2021	LGU's MOOE	Group involvement was done properly in campus journalism
	Araling Panlipunan Quiz Bee	Promote high performance of the child.	Quiz Bee should be conducted from Grades I-VI	Aug 2021	LGU's MOOE	Quiz Bee Conducted successfully
	Conducting School Leadership Training	Develop potential leaders	Pupils' initiative Turo mo, Babasa ako	Sept 2021	LGU's PTA	The training was conducted accordingly.
Teachers' Development	Attending Master's Degree	Upgrade learnings and professional's growth	Teachers attend Master's Degree	June-Mar 2021	Individual Expense	Permitted and Complied
	Attending Seminars	Uplift and update to the new trends of learning	Attend professional development learning	Oct 2021 Inset	Individual Expense	Teachers Attended Seminars
Curriculum Development	Enhancing the curriculum Guide in K to 12 and BEC	Enhance the MELCs used in K to 12	Monitor and enrich the curriculum	June-March 2021	MOOE, Individual Expense	Localized and Contextualized MELCS
Physical Facilities	Classroom structuring	Promote child-friendly classroom	Upgrade the pupils' learning using interactive multimedia facilities	June-March 2021	MOOE, Stakeholders	Well-Equipped to the new trend materials
	Using Multimedia Projector and other New Trends Materials	Use/implement the new trend materials in the teaching-learning process approach		June-March 2021	MOOE, Stakeholders	

3

CHAIRMAN OF A SPECIAL COMMITTEE

A teacher who served as Chairman of a Special Committee (DepEd programs not included) such as curriculum review committee to prepare instructional materials, Committee to prepare general school program and discharge the work effectively shall get a maximum of 12 points if fully documented. A special committee refers to the task requiring technical knowledge.

The chair of the school committee entails far more than sitting over meetings. It requires time, technical skills, organizational qualities, management skills, interpersonal skills, and understanding of the school's ethical responsibilities. The chairing of the school committee has a particular range of challenges. An efficient chair can easily influence the Committee to address these obstacles, concentrate on student performance, and meet the school's mission, vision, and priorities.

The overall objective of the school committee is the ongoing improvement of academic performance. Also, successful school special committees play a vital role in promoting student success.

The Curriculum Study Committee may provide work on the intervention or improvement program in various learning, assessment, supervision, and evaluation.

The Committee to prepare instructional materials may include the development of instructional materials, the development of evaluation instruments, questionnaires, test materials, and instructional materials' quality assurance.

The Committee to prepare the school program can include the school/grade/year/teacher work schedule program. A special committee's chairmanship is set up to support the specific DepEd (CO/RO/DO) program to enhance school performance.

Claim for Chairmanship of a Special Committee

1. Credited for curriculum/instructional materials
   - Modules, guides, manuals, lesson plans
   - Worksheets, exercises, workbooks

2. Credited for school programs are: testing, reading, math, remedial and enrichment programs
   Documents:
   - Memorandum on the organization of the special committee signed by the School Head and PSDS
   - Certification for serving as chairman of a special committee corroborated by 5 teachers and duly notarized
   - Project proposal signed by School Head
   - Action Plan signed by School Head and PSDS
   - Copy of the outputs - curriculum/ instructional materials or prepared program
   - Write-up of accomplishments signed by School Head and PSDS

Traits of an Effective Chairman of a Special Committee

- Decides to commit to a vision of high standards for student success and quality education and identifies concrete priorities for that vision.

- Has clear standard views and ideas about what learners should understand about the curriculum and its capacity to educate all learners to a greater extent.

- Responsibility driven, investing less time on organizational problems and more time working on policies to boost academic success.

- Has a working partnership with staff and the community and create a clear contact framework to engage and involve all internal and external partners in the growth and accomplishment of school priorities.

- Accepts and tracks data, even though the information is disappointing, and it is used to drive performance development.

- Participates in project management to create mutual awareness, principles, and commitments for development initiatives.

Documents Required

✓ Designation as Chairman of Special Work/Committee or a copy of List of Working Committees. **3pts**

✓ Evidences/Proofs of Implementation of Action Plan/Calendar of Activities (Pictures, Accomplishment Reports, Testimonies) **3pts**

✓ Impact/contributions of the project to beneficiaries. (Points to be given shall be based on the attainment of the objectives stated in the proposal. One point for every objective attained, maximum of 6 points.) **6pts**

Sample Designation of a Chairman
of a Special Committee

To   : **JUAN DELA CRUZ**
         Teacher III

From : School Head
Subject: Designation as Chairman of a Special
          Committee to prepare instructional materials

Date   : January 21, 2021

Sir:

     In addition to your effective function as Teacher III and in the exigency of the service, you are designated as Chairman to prepare instructional materials in English (Gr. I-VI) effective January 21, 2021.

     As chairman of a special committee, you are tasked to:

1. determine the least learned competencies;
2. develop curriculum materials;
3. ascertain the content validity of the developed instructional materials;
4. identify the level of acceptability of the instructional materials in terms of usefulness and sustainability; and
5. test and try out the effectiveness of the developed instructional materials.

For information and guidance.

____
School Head

4

EDUCATIONAL RESEARCH

Research is essential to your school's growth and can allow you to get the position you're dreaming of.

A teacher who initiated or headed an educational research activity duly approved by education authorities, either for improvement of instruction or for community development for teacher welfare, shall get a maximum of 12 points if fully documented.

Research shall be either action-based research or applied research.

Research proposals had to be recognized/noted/authorized by the School Head/School Research Committee (SRC), reviewed by the Schools Division Research Committee (SDRC). They were recommended and approved by the Assistant Schools Division Superintendent (ASDS) and the Schools Division Superintendent (SDS).

The completed study shall have a terminal write-up properly accepted and approved by the SDRC and recommended and approved by the ASDS and SDS, respectively.

Research themes shall be consistent with the CO/RO/SDO research policy and with the level of governance.

Thesis and dissertations shall not be credited to points. For individual research, a credit of 12 points shall be issued. For group claims, points shall be distributed evenly among researchers, except for research funded under the Basic Education Research Fund (BERF), in which case all members shall earn 12 points each.

Research Themes in the New Normal

Theme 1: Teaching & Learning

The research agenda looks into strategies, best practices, and facilitating and hindering factors relative to five sub-themes: instruction, curriculum, learners, assessment, and learning outcome. Main topics under Teaching and Learning include, but not limited to, the following:

Learning Delivery Modalities

- Relevance of Most Essential Learning Competencies (MELCs)
- Teaching and Learning Resources
- Strategies for K to 3
- Students' Achievement/Competencies
- Teachers' Content Knowledge
- Students' Attitude towards Assessment
- Teaching Reading/Numeracy
- Values
- Behaviors
- Career Paths/Tracks/Goals
- Personality Traits
- Affective/Psychological Traits
- Self-efficacy
- ICT Applications
- School-Home Linkage
- Kto12 Graduates
- Inclusive Education Programs (IPEd, Madrasah, SPEd, Special Interest Programs)
- ALS

- Contextualizing Learning Strategies and Modalities
- Culture, Arts & Literature
- 21st Century Skills
- MTB-MLE
- Flexible Learning Options
- Spiral Progression
- Assessment
- Test Construction
- Environmental Awareness
- Climate Change Adaptation and Mitigation
- Student Retention, Transition
- Gender Sensitivity

Theme 2: Child Protection

DepEd's learner-centered approach recognizes that a child's condition can significantly affect the achievement of learning outcomes. While the Department may not have the direct mandate and resources to address many of the social, economic, and personal issues of learners, it is committed to ensuring their well-being, particularly in situations where harm can occur in school or disrupt their studies. The Department's commitment warrants a separate section on Child Protection, particularly to address reported incidents of bullying, teenage pregnancy, addictive behaviors, and child labor. While laws and policies are in place to address these, there is a need to assess previous interventions' effectiveness and the potential of new approaches to protect learners in schools better. Main topics under Child Protection include, but are not limited to, the following:

- Mental Health
- Data Privacy and Protection
- Prevalence
- Teenage Pregnancy
- Bullying
- Drugs
- Child Labor
- Gambling
- HIV/AIDS
- Reproductive Health

Theme 3: Human Resource Development

As DepEd is the nation's largest bureaucracy, various strategies must be developed to nurture the vast human capital involved in delivering basic education. Research questions will delve into three subthemes: (1) teaching and non-teaching qualifications and hiring; (2) career development; and (3) employee's welfare. The primary focus is given to teachers due to their frontline role in reaching out to learners. Research questions probe into the teachers' existing qualifications and competency requirements vis-a'-vis the needs of the K to 12 and special education programs such as ALS. The topics extend to teacher education institutions, particularly on ways to upgrade pre-service preparation and DepEd's Role in providing continuous quality training. Similarly, developing the support structure of DepEd through its non-teaching personnel is an important area of inquiry. Key topics under Teaching and Non- Teaching Qualifications and Hiring included, but are not limited to, the following:

- Professional Development of Teachers / School Heads for Multiple Learning Delivery Modalities
- Mental Health
- Teaching and Non-Teaching Qualifications and Hiring
- Career Development
- Employee's Welfare
- Performance Appraisal System
- Performance Appraisal System
- Mentoring Support
- Values Orientation
- Research Aptitude
- Upskilling and Reskilling of Teachers
- Gender and Development

Theme 4: Governance

Managing the largest bureaucracy towards educating the nation's future requires efficient and effective operations. The Governance theme of the Research Agenda, which covers planning, finance, program management, transparency and accountability, and evaluation, underscores DepEd's commitment to ensure that its structure, systems, and processes contribute to the achievement of basic education outcomes. The Department has already provided internal guidance (DepEd Order 13, s. 2015) to develop effective and efficient policies. With this in place, DepEd's next concern is to ensure that these policies are implemented and translated into appropriate programs. Because it governs a very large sector with complex interrelationships, it often encounters challenges in its Planning process. This section deals with standards and policies that ensure the achievement of the Department's goals. Key topics under Governance included, but are not limited to, the following:

- Managing Schools in the New Normal
- Data Management
- Finance
- Crisis Leadership
- Internal Systems and Processes
- Innovative Programs
- Program Monitoring and Evaluation
- Alternative Work Arrangement
- Program Sustainability
- Transparency & Accountability
- Evaluation
- Customer's Satisfaction
- Waste Management
- Parental Engagement
- Safety and Health Management Systems
- Stakeholders Partnership and Engagement
- Procurement
- Impact Assessment
- Quality Assurance Systems
- Policy and legislation studies
- Equipment and Infrastructure

Note:

Research that will be conducted should convey information on raising the quality of education and anchored as well on the four pillars of Sulong Edukalidad: (1) K to 12 Curriculum review and update; (2) Improvement of the learning environment; (3) Teachers' upskilling and reskilling; and (4) Engagement of stakeholders for support and collaboration.

Outline of a Research Proposal

The research shall use the DepEd prescribed outline below for the research proposal. The research proposal should contain the following:

Title

The title of the research proposal must be brief and concise, researchable, novel indicates possibilities for further research, and time for completing the study is possible.

Rationale

It includes the rationale for the research and relevant, social, policy, or practice context for the study. The introduction should explain why the research study is being undertaken (e.g. to answer a question about a specified problem in education) and how the results could be used in action planning and/or policy formulation and development.

Hypothesis

The null hypothesis is commonly used by the proponent in research paper proposals because it is a denial of the existence of the difference of the effect which is easy to reject and accept.

Significance of the Study

The significance of the study is presented with either an inductive or a deductive perspective. When using an inductive perspective, the researcher discusses the importance of the study from particular to the general. He starts discussing the importance of the study from target beneficiaries, the researcher himself, to the people in the locality, province, region, and nation. When a deductive perspective is used, the researcher presents the importance of the study starting from the general to the particular- from the national level down to the regional, provincial and municipal levels, to the researcher, and to the target beneficiaries.

The researcher should prove that the study has important contributions in relation to: (a) solving the problem and need; (b) bridging a knowledge gap; (c) improving social, economic, and health conditions of the people; (d) enriching research instruments, methods and strategies; and (e) supporting government thrusts.

Scope and Limitations

This is the coverage of the research in terms of location, time, respondents, etc., inherent design or methodology parameters that can restrict the scope of the research findings and are outside the control of the researcher.

Research Methodology

It contains details of how the research will be conducted.

a. *Respondents* – The researcher has to explain how and where the respondents will be taken from. It can be either a total population if the population is small, less than 100, or a sample survey if the population is large, 100 or more.

b. *Sampling* – The details should be provided about who will participate in the research; the number of people and the characteristics of those who will participate in the research; and how will the sample be selected and recruited.

c. *Intervention* - it must have sufficient technical quality to resolve the problem. It should meet the criteria of cost, time, reliability, efficiency, and adaptability. It should meet minimum resistance from those who will have to implement it. The teacher-researcher should perceive the intervention as something they are prepared to invest time and energy in. The level of risk is not too high. The intervention should have potential benefits.

d. *Instrument* – The research instrument can be a questionnaire, a test, an interview, an observation schedule, or a rating scale. Each part of the instrument must be clearly stated described by the teacher-researcher. Suggestions, corrections, and refinement of the draft of the questionnaire must be explained thoroughly. The different individuals involved in the corrections and refinement of the questionnaire must be mentioned. After it is refined, testing the validity and reliability of the teacher-made instrument, questionnaire, must be done.

For validity, five experts in the field of study must be requested to go over the research instrument to test the validity.

For reliability, the teacher-researcher will use either test-retest, split-half, parallel- forms, or internal consistency.

If the research instrument is both valid and reliable, it is now ready to be administered to the subjects of the study.

e. *Data collection* – The various instruments and procedures for data collection should be outlined and extensively discussed. In here, the researcher proceeds to ask permission and approval from the Schools Division Research Committee where the subjects are employed. Once permitted, the researcher administers the research instrument to the respondents of the study. The date of the administration of the questionnaire, retrieval date, and percentage retrieval of the research instrument must be stated.

f. *Ethical Issues* – Identification of ethical concerns that could possibly emanate from the conduct of the research, and an elaborate discussion on how to prevent these from taking place. It can include, but not limited to the following: right to conduct a study or investigation to answer a question; securing free prior and informed consent from respondents; issues of confidentiality and anonymity; written approval for use of materials with copyright (e.g. secondary data sets, data collection tools).

g. *Plan for Data Analysis* – It indicates how the data will be analyzed and reported; it should specify the qualitative and/or quantitative methods that will be used in analyzing the data gathered for the research. The statistical tools used to answer the specific research questions of the study must be described and the formula must be explained. The level of significance either 1% or 5% must be stated to determine the significance of the findings.

Work Plan

It contains the research timelines – when will the project begin and how long will it take for it to be completed; include time estimates for each step in the research process (e.g. 5 days, 2 weeks).

Cost Estimates

It includes detailed research cost, broken down per research task, activity, and/or deliverable. It can be further grouped into tranches for easier reference of the Evaluation Committee.

Plans for Dissemination and Advocacy

It indicates how the results of the research will be cascaded to the intended user of the research findings (e.g. presentation in conferences, etc.).

References

Using APA referencing, provide in-text of work and reference list consistently and accurately.

Documents Required

- ✓ Approved research proposal. **2pts**

- ✓ Evidences / Proofs of research activities undertaken. (Data collection, Analysis and Interpretation, and Research Report) **2pts**

- ✓ Impact / Contributions of the Research Activity. (Points to be given shall be based on the attainment of the objectives stated in the proposal. One point for every objective attained, maximum of 4 points.) **4pts**

- ✓ Project was adopted by other schools / districts / division. **4pts**
  From the 4 points, the following distribution scheme shall apply. If project was adopted at the:

  a) school and district level – 1pt
  b) school, district and division level - 2pts
  c) school, district, division and regional level – 3pts
  d) school, district, division, regional and national level – 4pts

Note: The candidate receives just half of the allocated points per criteria for inclusion as a participant of such activity. Mere analysis of data is not considered an action research, and shall not be awarded a point.

Supporting documents: Approved letter to conduct research or Certificate of Approval, Research Manuscript, and letter of acceptance.

Sample Research Proposal

Digital Spelling Calendar As An Innovation To Improve Spelling Level of Students in the New Normal Set up

Rationale

Spelling, like speaking and writing, is an expressive skill. Frith (2008) stressed that reading and writing can be meaningless without spelling. In other words, spelling is the foundation for writing. In the 21st-century, all students must learn spellings for new topic words, for frequently used irregular words, regular words, and word families containing known letters and letter clusters. As part of the K-12 framework in the Philippines for 21st-century competencies, spelling skills include the expression of ideas accurately in written forms and uses a variety of strategies to write informational and literary compositions. Research shows that many students have problems in writing because they are not able to spell words correctly (Meriem, 2010). The differences between the standards of performance expected in the curriculum and the actual performance of the students prompted the researcher to identify the problem and seek intervention to remedy it.

After giving a series of spelling tests to grade 4 class in ABC Elementary School, students' inability to spell words in English was evident. Based on the gathered data, only 5 have proficiency level and 27 out of 32 students have below proficiency level in spelling.

The teacher-researcher has also found out that in writing composition in English, 10 or 31% of the students used misspelled words but conveying different meanings like in homonyms. Thirteen or 41% of the pupils write words as it sounds without considering the short and long a's, e's, i's, o's, and u's. Sixteen or 50% have difficulties in writing the rearrangement of ei, ie, ou, uo, ous, and uous and spelling patterns of al, il, le, ure, sher, and age and 15 or 47% find it difficult to write schwa n, /shun/, /zwah/ sounds. Moreover, 32 or 100% of the students have difficulty in writing the correct words derived from foreign languages like German, French, Latin and slang sounds, like a reservoir, repertoire, denouement, and others.

Pieces of literature on spelling difficulties were summed up to identify the factors involved in spelling problems of the students. The following were the causes: (1) dominance of mother tongue in the early years; (2) lack of support at home; and (3) inappropriate use of teaching pedagogy that focus on the development of spelling proficiency.

The dominance of the mother tongue has a direct influence on spelling English words. Mendoza (2014) stressed that errors made in spelling are due to the difference in the sound system and spelling symbols between mother tongue and English. This manifests in the form of incorrect pronunciation of students before they spell the words.

Another immediate cause of the existence of low spelling ability was the lack of support at home. This was brought by the absence of culture in taking time to spell to their children. Recent research shows that spelling words are largely determined by parental practices, particularly school-aged children (Biemiller 2014). Children mainly spell words when parents are used to having spelling activities at home.

The presence of students having low spelling proficiency in English was also greatly affected by the inappropriate use of teaching pedagogy that focused on the development of spelling proficiency. On the surface level, teachers adopted the *"Kung ano ang bigkas, siya ang baybay."* which was introduced in some learning areas in the early years. However, a deeper analysis revealed that they were more complacent with traditional strategies in the classroom setting. Teachers lack either the expertise in spelling or the expertise in teaching spelling (Mountford, 2014). As a result, learners have devised personal strategies in learning to spell by copying whole words, by rote, or by looking up spelling in the dictionary. Udu (2013) found out that appropriate teaching pedagogy in teaching spelling hold the promise of arousing the interest of school children and improving the way children learn the skill of spelling.

It is on this premise that the action research project was conceptualized based on the belief that using appropriate teaching intervention has the potential to improve students' spelling performance.

Research Questions

The main purpose of this action research is to improve the spelling performance of grade 4 students at ABC Elementary School using Digital Spelling Calendar for the school year 2020-2021.

Specifically, it sought to answer the following research questions:

1. How is the spelling performance of grade 4 students differ in the pre-test and post-test?
2. Is there a significant difference in the spelling performance of students during the administration of pretest and post-test?
3. What are the student-respondents' perceptions towards the use of Four-Quadrant Approach in the English spelling class?
4. What recommendations can be proposed to maximize the use Four-Quadrant Approach (FQA) as an intervention to improve students' spelling performance?

Hypotheses

The hypothesis of the study will be tested in null form at .05 level of significance.

There is no significant difference between the pre-test and posttest results of the experimental group.

Significance of the Study

The teacher-researcher believes that the results of the study will be of benefit to the following:

DepEd Officials. Through the result of this action research study, the DepEd officials will be guided in the formulation of school programs, projects, and activities.

The School Administrators. The findings of the action research study can guide them on how to plan activities related to the implementation of the provisions for in-service pedagogical training.

The Elementary School Teachers. The result of the action research study can help them enhance learning facilitation through selecting appropriate pedagogical strategy as an opportunity to create local change in the classroom setting.

The Teacher-Researcher. Through this study, the researcher will be able to effectively perform his duties and responsibilities in line with the exercise of his authority on how to improve students' spelling performance in English.

Other Researchers. This study can serve as a springboard to a similar study on a wider range of locales and longer times.

Respondents

The participants of the study will be 10 males and 11 females of grade 4 special science of ABC Elementary School who are identified to have an internet connection at home for the SY 2020-2021. Their mean average in English is 82% in the previous grade level.

Sampling Method

Participants will be selected through purposive sampling technique. In this technique, a desired number of sample units is selected purposely that depends upon the objective of the study so that the important items representing the true characteristics of the population are included in the sample.

Interventions

Digital Spelling Calendar is an intervention originally developed by the teacher-researcher to improve the students' spelling performance in the experimental group. In this approach, students have to spell words based on the grade four K-12 content pedagogy. A set of twenty-one spelling words will be given to students and have spelling activity each Monday, Tuesday, Wednesday and Thursday afternoon. These words are found in the passages of stories and included in the discussion of each lesson in English 4. Initially, the teacher-researcher has to show a square with four quadrants on any selected social media platform. Students have also individual copies of the square for them to keep given during the distribution of self-learning modules. The teacher- researcher will instruct the students that they have to complete the spelling challenge for all four squares. At the beginning of spelling instruction, the teacher-researcher will emphasize the phonetic nature of spelling for the students learn to spell words based on the phonemic processing.

Each Monday, after reading the text, students will be asked to type the spelling words in alphabetical order in the FB chatbox. Williams (2015) stated that once a child has mastered putting the letters in alphabetical order, children become confident to spell words because of the opportunity to build their skill in knowing the first letter of the given words.

Each Tuesday, students will be asked to break the spelling word up into syllables. Syllable breakdown is a strategy to help children spell long words. According to Reed (2015) when spelling instruction emphasizes the syllabic patterns, it will improve students' spelling ability thus contributes to students becoming better overall readers and writers.

Each Wednesday, students will be asked to type each spelling word using a different color in MS Word. According to Rosen (2015), using colors in spelling is considered a marker and milestone in a child's cognitive process and is often part of familiarizing the spelling of words. Newing (2015) stated the idea that drill in spelling using colors helps to create the cognitive linkbetween visual clues and words.

Each Thursday, students will be asked to count the letters in each spelling word and type the words in order from least to most letters. Seril (2014) asserted that letter counting has a strong influence on children's ability to spell words. Likewise, Gaske (2015) stated that the number of letters in a word the brain receives heighten high retention of words.

The implementation of this intervention will last for three months from November 2020 to February 2021 from Monday to Thursday for about 30 minutes a day between 11:00 to 11:30 in the morning.

Digital Spelling Calendar is anchored on Sigmund Freud's Developmental Stage Theory in education. This theory indicates that students' orthographic knowledge aligns very consistently with their current stage of spelling development across a range of activities. (Freud et al., 1953).

Instruments

The first instrument is a pre- and post-test tests, both consisting the same 100-item spelling words were used to determine the significant difference in the spelling performance of the experimental group. Validity of the test was assured through 5 subject experts of English. The 5% items were deleted and replaced as a result of this judgment. Likewise, spelling competencies in grade 4 were distributed in the table of specifications for content validity. The test was trialed with other students from other sections. Reliability of the post-test was assured through a research experts and it found to be 0.91. Respondents will be given a 20-minute length of time to complete each spelling activities.

The second instrument is the in-depth interviews which comprised 5 general questions and some probing questions to elicit respondents' answer to "what", "why", and "how" of the use of Digital Spelling Calendar in spelling instruction. The in-depth interviews included answers to the following questions: Do you have any difficulty in learning English spelling words? Do you like Digital Spelling Calendar? Why or why not? Can you give some examples of activities in the Digital Spelling Calendar you like and dislike? How often do you want to use Digital Spelling Calendar in learning English spelling words? Do you think it fun to learn English spelling words though Digital Spelling Calendar? Which approach do you prefer, the new one using

Digital Spelling Calendar or the traditional one? Why?

The third instrument was the teacher-researcher's field notes. This was used during the implementation of the intervention to record descriptive and reflective information. The field notes included answers to the following questions: How successful the respondents interact with the spelling activities? Did the respondents follow the rules and behave properly? Are there any unexpected problems arise during the implementation of the intervention? If there is, transcribe the situation.

Data Collection Procedure

Initially, the teacher-researcher asked and secured permission from the Schools Division Research Committee (SDRC) of Dep-Ed XYZ province prior the conduct of the study.

Then, the whole sample was given a pre-spelling test before the implementation of the intervention. The group will be taught with the Digital Spelling Calendar. The treatment of the group will be for a period of three months. At the end of treatment, post-spelling test will be administered to check the spelling performance.

Following the experiment, three students will randomly be selected by drawing their numbers from the class list and participated in a 20-minute in-depth interview individually. The interview questions will be open-ended and translated in Ilokano as the respondents would feel more comfortable and express themselves better in their first language. All three interviews will be transcribed for analysis.

Scores (out of 100 points) of the two pairs of the test were entered into paired samples t-tests, whereas the interview transcriptions were analyzed and interpreted by the interviewer and the teacher-researcher.

Ethical Considerations

The teacher-researcher set ethical standards against the fabrication and falsifying data. The teacher-researcher secured assent from the School Head and informed consent from respondents (see Appendix D). The teacher-researcher carefully explained the research process and provided information on the research with its aims and objectives without influencing the students" responses. Moreover, this study claimed confidentiality and anonymity to the data of the students. Likewise, cross-referencing related literature and studies were observed using the APA style of citing authorities.

Data Analysis

To indicate how the data was analyzed and reported, the following specifications for the quantitative and qualitative methods were used in analyzing the data gathered from the research.

For Research Problem Number 1. To describe the difference in spelling performance of grade 4 students in their pre-test and post-test, mean and percentage will be employed.

For Research Problem Number 2. To determine if there is a significant difference in the spelling performance of students during the pretest and post-test, paired t-test will be used

For Research Problem Number 3. To describe the respondents' perceptions towards the use of Digital Spelling Calendar in the English spelling class, thematic analysis will be used on the interview data.

Work plan

The table indicates the specific activities that will be undertaken by the teacher-researcher in relation to the collection of data. It contains the research timelines – when will the project will start and how long it will it take to be completed. It also includes time estimates for each step in the research process.

Work plan		Resources	
Activities	**Timeline**	**Person**	**Physical**
A. Conceptualization of the Research Proposal			
A.1 Draft the proposal.	October 10-16, 2020 (7 days)	Teacher-Researcher	Books. Journals, internet materials
A. 2 Validate Research Instrument.	October 17-23, 2020 (6 days)	Teacher-Researcher, Students	MS Excel
A. 3 Submit the proposal for acceptance.	October 24, 2020 (1 day)	Teacher-Researcher, SDRC	Research proposal
B. Implementation of the Approved Research Proposal			
B. 1 Meet the School Head and parents. B. 2 Present the title, coverage, objectives, and significance of the study. B. 3 Class Orientation.	October 31-November 3, 2020 (4 days)	Teacher-Researcher, School Head, Parents, Student-respondents	Salient parts of the research proposal
B. 4 Conduct a pre-spelling test to determine the baseline data of the respondents.	November 4, 2020 (1 day)	Teacher-Researcher, Student respondents	Pre-spelling test form
B. 5 Implement the intervention: Digital Spelling Calendar B. 6.1 Prepare the spelling words. 6.2 Come up with spelling matrix. 6.3 Conduct spelling activities. 6.4 Fill out Teacher's Field Notes	November 14, 2020 to February 10, 2021 (3 months)	Teacher-Researcher, Student-respondents	FQA template Chart, list of spelling words, teachers' field notes

B. 7 Conduct a post-spelling test to the respondents.	February 16, 2021 (1 day)	Teacher-Researcher, Student-respondents	Post-spelling test form
B. 8 Interview 3 randomly selected students and let them participate in the in-depth interview individually.	February 17, 2021 (1 day)	Teacher-Researcher, Student-respondents, Interviewer	Interview form
B. 9 Evaluate the effects of the Digital Spelling Calendar	February 20-23, 2021 (3 days)	Teacher-Researcher,	Pre-and Post-spelling test forms, result of the interview
B. 10 Reflect on the interventions used.	February 24-28, 2021 (5 days)	Teacher-Researcher	Result of the findings
B. 11 Write the final action research report.	March 3-9, 2021 (5 days)	Teacher-Researcher	Result of the findings
B. 12 Submit the final report for approval.	March 10, 2021 (1 day)	Teacher-Researcher, SDRC	Final copy of the research
B. 13 Submit the bound copy to SDRC	March 7, 2021 (1 day)	Teacher-Researcher, SDRC	bound copy of the research
C. Results Dissemination			
Disseminate the research result to school InSeT, Division, Regional, National and International Research Congress	November to December 2021	Teacher-Researcher, Teachers, SDRC, leaders from Educational Institutions	Final copy of the research, leaflets, salient parts of the research

Cost Estimates		
Activities	**Particulars**	**Amount**
A. Conceptualization		
1. Supply and Materials	1 ream bond paper, 1 set of printer ink, 5 folders	1,760
2. Online Library Searches	at least 20 times online searches	500
3. Reproduction of the Pre-Survey Instrument, Teacher Field Notes & Consent and Assent Forms	32 copies each	310
4. Printing of the Research proposal	5 copies of approx. 45 pages each	1,180

B.	Implementation		
1. Supply and Materials	1 ream bond paper, 1 set of printer inks, 1 record book, 1 box clips, 15 folders		1,655
2. Online Library Searches	at least 20 times online searches		500
3. Local Transportation	Consultation with the SDRC and securing supply and materials, etc.		1,560
4. Reproduction of the Research Instruments	32 copies each		460
5. Reproduction of the Final Research Paper	5 copies of approx. 60 pages each		2,010
6. Binding of the Final Research Copy	8 binds		500
C.	Results Dissemination		
1. School InSeT/SLAC sessions	Production for reproduction of related materials		1,890
2. Division or Regional Research Congress, National or international Research Conference	Production for reproduction of related materials		1,990
		Total	14,315

Plans for Dissemination and Advocacy

Upon the approval of this action research, the teacher-researcher will be presenting the approved action research in the school In-Service Training (InSeT), division, regional, national and international research congress. Furthermore, the proponent will ask the School Head to institutionalize the result of the action research within the school-based academic programs.

DECLARATION OF ABSENCE OF CONFLICT OF INTEREST
(Annex 3 of DO No. 16, s. 2017)

1. I,_______________________, understand that conflict of interest refers to situations in which financial or other personal considerations may compromise my judgment in evaluating, conducting, or reporting research.

2. I hereby declare that I do not have any personal conflict of interest that may arise from my application and submission of my research proposal. I understand that my research proposal may be returned to me if found out that there is conflict of interest during the initial screening as per DO No. 16, s. 2017.

3. Further, in case of any form of conflict of interest (possible or actual) which may inadvertently emerge during the conduct of my research, I will duly report it to the research committee for immediate action.

4. I understand that I may be held accountable by the Department of Education and (insert grant mechanism) for any conflict of interest which I have intentionally concealed.

Proponent:_________________________________

Signature:_________________________________

DECLARATION OF ANTI-PLAGIARISM
(Annex 3 of DO No. 16, s. 2017)

1. I, _________________________understand that plagiarism is the act of taking and using another's ideas and works and passing them off as one's own. This includes explicitly copying the whole work of another person and/or using some parts of their work without proper acknowledgment and referencing.

2. I hereby attest to the originality of this research proposal and has cited properly all the references used. I further commit that all deliverables and the final research study emanating from this proposal shall be of original content. I shall use appropriate citations in referencing other works from various sources.

3. I understand that violation from this declaration and commitment shall be subject to consequences and shall be dealt with accordingly by the Department of Education and (insert grant mechanism).

Proponent:_________________________________
Signature:_________________________________
Date:_________________________________

5

COORDINATOR OF COMMUNITY PROJECT

The community project is community-based, not school-based, and sponsored by any of the following: LGU or Barangay, RIC, other government agencies, or a non-government organization.

A teacher who served as coordinator of community project/activity or a program of another agency, or coordinator of a rural service improvement activity in a community such as a tree planting, clean and green, feeding, nutrition, agro-industrial, sports fest, centennial, city/town fiesta, cultural shows, etc. for at least two years shall get a maximum of 12 points in the ranking if fully documented. It must be a program or a project continuously implemented for two (2) years.

The function of a Community Project Coordinator

The Community Project Coordinator provides community development, campaigns for community members to help clients' needs with resources and referral programs, and encourages understanding of social issues and developments within the community.

Roles and Responsibilities

- Responsibility for the creation, coordination, and implementation of activities.

- Establish and execute policy goals, objectives, and evaluations of results.

- Assess and guide the required service/delivery method, e.g., Knowledge, facilitation, preparation, mediation coaching, involvement, or referral.

- Demonstrate a positive awareness of the values and strategies of community development.
- Consult and communicate with members of the community/group.
- Coordinate complex tasks as needed.
- Assist in the creation and management of appropriate collaborations and relationships.
- Build and sustain an effective working relationship that is responsive to individual differences and different communities.
- Perform group consultation or interaction and build partnerships;
- Build and maintain close ties with key stakeholders.

Skills Needed

- Understanding the values and principles of community development
- Verbal and written communication skills
- Capacity to communicate successfully with people, organizations, and agencies
- Managing challenges, crisis intervention, and negotiating skills
- Capacity to balance a variety of goals
- Willingness to work with a large and varied customer community
- Good leadership qualities

Other Requirement

- Immunizations highly recommended in the "new normal"

Note:

- *Community projects are accomplished for the benefit of the community (purok, barangay, town, and not for the school).*

- *For outreach programs/activities where the applicant served as proponent/chairman, the maximum point to be given is 12 points regardless of the number of times of involvement.*

- *For outreach programs undertaken with other government agencies and private organizations/NGOs, these must have been documented in coordination with the school and the DepEd.*

Documents Required

✓ Official Designation from the head of the agency. **3pts**

✓ Evidences / proofs of implementation of Action Plan/Calendar of Activities (Pictures, Accomplishment report, testimonies) **3pts**

✓ Impact/contributions of the designation (Points to be given shall be based on the attainment of the objectives stated in the Action Plan/Work Plan. One point for every objective attained, maximum of 6 points.) **6pts**

Supporting documents shall be as follows:

- Designation as coordinator/project focal person/project proponent duly signed by the head/chair/president of the lead organization or sponsor.
- Project proposal/write-up and completion summary for the project duly approved by the concerned agency and approved/noted by the ASDS/SDS.
- A certificate of commendation/recognition granted to the proponent or the project participant can be included.

Other Documents Required

1. Barangay resolution for the Designation
2. Approved Project Proposal by the Barangay/Agency
3. Progress Report for two (2) years
4. Letter of Invitation
5. Certification from the agency

Sample Designation for a Community Project

Republic of the Philippines
Province of ABC– Municipality of XYZ
Barangay Maligaya

OFFICE OF THE BARANGAY CHAIRMAN

January 1, 2021

Special Order of MR JUAN DELA CRUZ

TO: Barangay officials &
Constituents
Brgy. Agricultural Technologist

To maintain good governance in a healthy and sound environment, JUAN DELA CRUZ is now appointed as COORDINATOR OF THE PROJECT BERDE. This clean and green project will run from January 2021 to January 2023.

In conjunction with his specific assignment, Mr. Dela Cruz is advised to coordinate immediately with the officials and constituents of this barangay to implement all the clean-up and greening activities.

This order will take effect immediately.

—————————————————
Brgy. Chairman

Sample Proposal for a Community Project

Project Title: Project FOSTER (Fortification Of Surroundings Through Environmental Restoration)

Proponent: Juan Dela Cruz
Contact No: 0910-xxx-xxxx

Implementer: Brgy. Maligaya

Target Clienteles: People in the community of Barangay Maligaya, Brgy. Council

Pursuant to Republic Act (R.A.) No. 9512, entitled "An Act to Promote Environmental Education and for Other Purposes", the Department of Education (DepEd) urges all public and private schools to lead the role on environmental awareness by enhancing environmental education and by pursuing effective school-based activities that seek to preserve and protect the environment. Republic Act No. 9512 was enacted in view of the pressing global concerns and issues on the environment.

Barangay Maligaya is one of the premier barangays in the Municipality of XYZ. This barangay is considered to be one of the biggest barangays in the town. It also has the biggest population in the whole municipality. One of the effects of the population growth in the barangay is the generation of wastes. Some people dumped their garbage anywhere not knowing the bad effects to the environment and health of the people, especially to the school children. Some children got sick because of the polluted air they breathed in. This leads them to absences in their class that results to poor their performance. So there is a need to educate the people and take necessary actions to prevent this problem to worsen. Cleanliness in the environment contributes a lot in maintaining a clean and green surrounding. Cleaning and greening the community is simple but helpful ways of improving a healthy environment. This is the purpose of the proponent to ensure solid waste is managed in such a way that protects both public health and the environment.

Sample Proposal for a Community Project

In this age, of environmental concern individuals are outwardly interested in the healthy state of their surroundings. As populations increase and we become more connected with our environment and each other through global communication, commerce and transportation, that interest also increases. Our desire for a clean environment represents a powerful sense of destiny and hope for the future.

It wasn't too many years ago that the world has been reported to have a global warming in its different natural features, but also the degradation activity brought by the population which needs to sustain their life-like tree cutting for burning charcoal and firewood, this was among the many reasons which make us to interested not only to show you visitors the natural features we have but also to collaborate in preventing them from pollution and degradation, through planting the trees on barren land on the barangay.

The environment is the most important resource for life. We get water, power and oxygen from the environment. It helps to clear pollution and is a large habitat for animals. Earth is getting polluted by poisonous gases and fumes made by cars and factories. A clean environment is essential for healthy living. Air pollution can cause respiratory diseases and cancer, among other problems and diseases. Water pollution can lead to typhoid, diarrheal diseases, and other water-related diseases. Therefore, we should keep our environment clean and protected.

Objectives

1. To conduct the clean-up drive in the community;
2. To tap possible donors of seedlings for tree planting in the community;
3. To plant trees in the community;
4. To promote the proper concept of the 3R principle (Reduce, Reuse and Recycle) in the community through an information dissemination campaign;
5. To tap possible donors of the five (5) blue plastic barrel drums for proper waste segregation in the community; and
6. To highlight environment advocacy program by displaying RA 9003 tarpaulin in the community

Sample Proposal for a Community Project

Project Description Components

Project FOSTER is a clean and Green projected initiated by the proponent. The proponent together with the barangay officials will meet and talk about the different cleaning and greening activities to be undertaken during the implementation of the program.

4. 1. Mobilization and Organizing Implementation

Activities	Person Responsible	Roles and Responsibilities
Cleaning Project	Person A	Coordinates with the barangay for the clean-up drive
Tapping donors for seedlings	Person B	Tap potential donors for the seedlings for tree planting
Tree planting activity	Person C	In-charge in tree planting
Promoting 3Rs (Reduce, Reuse, Recycle)	Person D	Facilitate in the 3Rs activity
Tapping possible donors of the five (5) plastic barrel drums for proper waste segregation in the community	Person E	Tap possible donors of the five (5) blue plastic drums for proper waste segregation in the community
Posting of RA 9003 "Bawal Magtapon ng Basura"	Person F	In-charge in lay-outing and posting of the tarpaulins

    4.1.1. Inform the barangay officials and constituents about the project.

    4.1.2. Create working committees.

    4.1.3. Create guidelines for the proper implementation of the project.

4.2. Implementation of the Project

    4.2.1 Each team leader and barangay officials will work together for the realization of the above-cited objectives.

    4.3. Internal Monitoring and Evaluation

Sample Proposal for a Community Project

The program/activity will be monitored by each of the chairmen of the different committees. All activities will be documented and supported with photos.

Funding Requirement Scheme
Self-help & donations from friends
The project proponent shall tap financial support to NGO's, stakeholders from other agencies, and barangay officials for financial support for implementation of the project.

ACTIVITIES	COSTS	TOTAL
Conducting the clean-up drive in the community.	500	500
Tapping possible donors of seedlings for the tree planting in the community	1,000	1,000
Tree planting activity	500	500
Training of community households to promote the proper concepts of 3R principle (reduce, Reuse, and Recycle)	500	500
Tapping stakeholders to donate five (5) plastic barrel drums for proper waste segregation	1,000	1,000
Posting of RA 9003: "Bawal Magtapon ng Basura" in the community	500	500

Schedule of Activities

Activities	Time Frame	Human Resources Involved	Expected Outcome
Conducting the clean-up drive in the community.	January, April, July, October 2021-2022	-Proponent -Brgy. Council -Community Households -Purok Leader -Brgy Agriculturist -Volunteers	Conducted Clean and Green project in the community
Tapping potential donors of seedling for the tree planting	January – March 2021	-Proponent -Brgy. Council	Seedlings for the tree planting

Sample Proposal for a Community Project

Activities	Time Frame	Human Resources Involved	Expected Outcome
Tree planting activity	June 2021 & June 2022	-Proponent -Brgy. Council -Community Households -Purok Leader -Brgy Agriculturist -Volunteers	Planted trees in the community
Training of community households to promote the proper concepts of 3R principle (reduce, Reuse, and Recycle)	February 2021	-Proponent -Community Households -Purok Leader	Community households were trained on how to reduce, reuse and recycle waste materials in the community
Tapping stakeholders to donate five (5) barrel drums for proper waste segregation in the community	January-June 2021	-Proponent -Brgy. Council	Five (5) plastic drums for proper waste segregation in the community
Posting of RA 9003: "Bawal magtapon ng Basura" in the community	March 2021	-Proponent -Brgy. Council	Posted two (2) tarpaulins of RA 9003 in the community

Expected Outcome

The community project will be documented supported with relevant documents and pieces of evidence of outputs during the organization and implementation of the project to cover the project's progress and success.

6

IN-SERVICE TRAINING

A teacher who organized or managed a three-day (at least) in service activity at least at the District / Cluster (Secondary) level for Master Teacher 1 and Division level for Master Teacher 2 shall get a maximum point of 12 in the ranking if fully documented.

The InSeT participants are teachers/School Heads/parents/community or a combination of both groups.

In-service training (InSeT) in DepEd is a professional development activity for teachers to address shared problems faced in the classroom, led by the head of the school or the designated InSeT Leader.

The core facets of the process are continuous joint learning or problem-solving within a common field of mutual interest, self-directed learning, analytical practice contributing to action and self-assessment, and mutual expertise.

The goals of InSeT are as follows:

- To improve the teaching-learning process that will lead to better learning among students;
- To foster good teachers;
- To allow teachers to inspire each other to continually develop their material and teaching expertise, experience, skills, and attitudes; and
- To promote a professional spirit of cooperation between school administrators, students, and the community as a whole.

Contents of the Training

The nature of the training can be achieved by a needs assessment, the findings of which should assist the organizer in listing their target learning areas. Special focus must be put on some of the main aspects of the K to 12 Basic Education Curriculum. It is critical that the teacher-identified issues are aligned with the following specific areas of discussion that represent the features of the K to 12 Basic Education Curriculum as set out in the Republic Act (R.A.) No.10533, the Enhanced Basic Education Act of 2013 and the various policies of the DepEd:

- *Learner Diversity and Student Inclusion*

The diversity of learners is the reason behind all education processes. Teachers have a key role to play in developing learning experiences that lead to the diversity of learners. It underlines the value of teachers' knowledge and comprehension of, and appreciation for, the attributes and experiences of learners. Teachers who embrace diversity in their classrooms adapt and vary their teaching to include all learners and promote unity in their classrooms. In addition, the integration of learners allows teachers to offer remedial guidance to those with learning disabilities. These strategies avoid disappointment and communicate student care to the teacher.

- *Content and Pedagogy*

   Content and performance standards and instructional skills must be learned by the teachers so that they can prepare activities, provide instruction efficiently, and measure the learning that has resulted from their teaching.

- *Assessment and Reporting*

   Any teacher should understand how to develop a learning-centered evaluation policy for the K to 12 Curriculum. Conversations about instruction can necessarily involve approaches to measure the learning of students and how data from the formative assessment will enhance future lessons.

- *21st Century Skills and ICT Integration*

   Teachers must improve lessons with easy integration techniques using Information and Communication Technology (ICT) that are suitable for learners' growth. Instruction and evaluation systems can be made more interactive with ICT that teachers can incorporate with the tools and equipment provided in their classrooms.

- *Curriculum Contextualization, Localization, and Indigenization*

   Teachers understand and respond to opportunities to connect teaching and learning in the classroom with the experiences, desires, and expectations of the broader school community and other primary stakeholders. By connecting new material to local events that students are familiar with, learning can be more effective and meaningful to them.

The localization of the program is a crucial aspect of the K to 12 Curriculum. The teaching guide and the materials of the learners can be changed to represent the special circumstances of a specific locality.

In addition to the topics laid out above, teachers can also take time to explore how their community connections will help the program and how teaching supports their own professional development. Besides, new and pressing topics or questions concerning teaching and learning need to be addressed.

In-Service Training Format

I.   Title

II.   Professional Standards Covered (Write the PPST, PPSSH, or PPSS domain/s), strand/s, indicator/s. If relative to program or policy implementation, write the title of policy/program to be discussed.

III.   Background/Rationale

IV.   Training Objectives

A.   Terminal Objective

B.   Enabling Objectives

V.   Proponent

VI.   Target Clienteles

VII.   Schedule of Activities

VIII.   Budgetary Requirements
    A. No. of Participants
    B. Budget/participant/Day
       Specify items of expenditures, e.g. AM snacks = Php 100.00 x 10 participants x 3 days = Php 3,000.00)

IX.   Funding Source

X.   Training Matrix

Time	Activity/Topic	Facilitator

XI.   Monitoring and Evaluation

XII.   Expected Output

Note:

- If MOOE Fund will be used, attach the approved Work Financial Plan signed by authorities
- DepEd Order No. 15, s. 2017, DepEd Order No. 2, s. 2018 and DBM Budget Circular 2007-1 may be used as a reference for budget allocation purposes.
- No DepEd personnel shall be entitled to an honorarium.
- For resource speakers outside DepEd, include the training matrix of the agency/institution he/she is associated with.
- Registration fees where teachers will shell out from their own pockets shall be strictly prohibited.

InSeT Evaluation Form

Title of Training: _________________
Venue: _________________
Date: _________________

Direction: Please rate the training based on the following statements by putting a check (/) mark on the appropriate boxes or as indicated in each item/indicator. All evaluations will be treated with confidentiality.

SA - Strongly Agree
A – Agree
D – Disagree
SD – Strongly Disagree

SESSIONS	SA	A	D	SD
1. Session started on time.				
2. Session ended on time.				
3. Topic was relevant to our work.				
4. Objectives of the session were achieved.				
5. Activities were congruent to objectives.				
6. Participants were engaged in activities.				
7. Learning materials were relevant.				
8. Time allotment was adequate.				
TRAINING VENUE				
1. Venue had adequate illumination.				
2. Venue had adequate ventilation.				
3. Venue was clean and hygienic.				
4. Venue had enough clean comfort rooms.				
5. Venue had enough facilities & space for needed activities.				
ACCOMMODATIONS				
1. Accommodation was comfortable.				
2. Accommodation had enough clean comfort rooms.				
3. Accommodation was close to the venue of the training.				
4. Accommodation was secure and safe.				
MEALS				
1. Menu offered generally healthy food with variety.				

	SA	A	D	SD
2. Menu considered dietary restrictions/requirements.				
3. Sufficient quantity.				
4. Served on time.				
PROGRAM MANAGEMENT				
1. Available when needed.				
2. Courteous.				
3. Efficient.				
4. Responsive to participants' needs.				

Write SA, A, D, SD for each speaker

SA – Strongly Agree
A – Agree
D – Disagree
SO – Strongly Disagree

Speaker 1 (S1)
Speaker 2 (S2)
Speaker 3 (S3)
Speaker 4 (S4)
Speaker 5 (S5)

Trainer/Facilitator	SA	A	D	SD
1. Exhibited full grasp/mastery of the topic				
2. Expressed ideas clearly, and explained complex ideas in easily understandable terms.				
3. Deepen learning by processing activities and asking stimulating questions.				
4. Was sensitive to the participants' mood.				
5. Used appropriate training needs.				

6. Helped meet the objectives of the training.				
7. Was responsive to questions and comments thus maintained a positive learning environment.				
8. Observed appropriate attire.				

Comments / Suggestions / Remarks for Improvement of the Training / Facilitator / Speaker / Program Management Team

____

____

____

____

Significant Learnings and Plan of Action

____

____

____

In-service Training Accomplishment Report Format

Program Title
Facilitators
Location and Venue
Duration
Date
No. of Participants
Executive Summary
Program Objectives
Program Schedule/Matrix/Design
Key Results
Resource Materials
M&E Analysis
(Based on the results of the End-of-Training Evaluation) Analysis should include:

- Results from the participants' evaluation of the training
- Results from the facilitators' review of the training
- Results from the training organizer review of the training
- Strengths and areas for improvement should be identified in this section

General Comments and Issues
In this section make any general comments about the training and identify any issues encountered in relation to:

- it's delivery
    -content of the training
    -delivery strategies
    -training materials

- its management
  -prior to delivery
  -during the training proper
- other issues

Recommendations

In this section, discuss any recommendations you may have to improve future programs. Suggestions may cover training management, facilitators, session guides, resource materials, other concerns.

Attachments:
- List of Participants
- Attendance Sheets (Arranged chronologically)
- M & E Results
- Breakdown of expenditures
- Photo Documentation

Documents Required

✓ Training Design/Program duly approved by the Schools Division Superintendent as recommended by the PSDS/EPS. **3pts**

✓ Evidences/proofs of implementation of Training Design (Pictures, Accomplishment Report, Attendance of Participants) **3pts**

✓ Impact/contributions of the designation. (Points to be given shall be based on the attainment of the objectives stated in the Training Design. One point for every objective attained, maximum of 6 points.) **6pts**

Note: *No points for co-organizer*

The supporting documents shall contain:
- Training design proposed and approved by the ASDS and SDS, respectively.
- Memorandum on the conduct of the InSeT
- Certificate of Appreciation can be included
- Certification of conduct of InSeT by the Head of School, verified by five teachers. Documents shall specifically demonstrate that the applicant is the InSeT Organizer.

Sample Proposal for In-Service Training

I. Title: District In-Service Training (InSeT) for teachers on Appropriate Teaching and Learning Resources and Processes in the New Normal Set-up of Education

II. Professional Standards Covered (Write the PPST, PPSSH or PPSS domain/s), strand/s, indicator/s. If relative to program or policy implementation, write the title of policy/program to be discussed.

1. Domain 1. Content Knowledge and Pedagogy
   Strand 1.5. Applying a range of teaching strategies to develop critical and creative thinking, as well as other higher order thinking skills
2. Domain 2. Learning Environment
   Strand 2.6. Managing learning behavior constructively by applying positive and non-violent discipline to ensure learning –focused environments
3. Domain 3. Diversity of Learners
   Strand 3.3. Designing, adapting and implementing teaching strategies that are responsive to learners with disabilities, giftedness and talents
4. Domain 4. Curriculum and Planning
5. Strand 4.5. Selecting, developing, organizing, and using diagnostic, formative, and summative strategies consistent with curriculum requirements
6. Domain 6. Community Linkages and Professional Engagement
   Strand 6.1. Complying with and implementing school policies and procedures consistently to foster harmonious relationships with learners, parents, and other stakeholders
7. Personal Growth and Professional Development
   Strand 7.3. Participating in professional networks to share knowledge and to enhance practice

Sample Proposal for In-Service Training

III. Background/Rationale

DepEd is mandated to fully support the continuing professional development of its teaching staff by the Republic Act No. 10533 or the Enhanced Basic Education Act of 2013. To fulfill this role, district and school teachers should be fully equipped with the relevant core and technical skills that will enable them to attend intensive training and support the continuing professional growth based on the principle of lifelong learning and the commitment of DepEd to the development of teachers and their potential for success in the profession.

This InSeT focuses on enhancing the skills needed by teachers on identified common topics. This ultimately contributes to their primary role as prime movers in the professional learning community. In this premise, ABC Elementary School will conduct 3-day InSeT through virtual and face-to-face modality by observing IATF protocols.

This program supports the Basic Learning Continuity Plan to train teachers with appropriate teaching and learning resources and processes to address the needs of learners in this pandemic. This InSeT will equip participants with new learning modalities and new ways to address the challenges of the CoViD-19 pandemic.

IV. Training Objectives

    A. Terminal Objective

        At the end of the InSeT, the participants are expected to be well capacitated educators even in this time of a pandemic

    B. Enabling Objectives

- Determine ways on how to cope up with challenges in the New Normal of Teaching and Learning;
- Develop understanding on the effective usage of ICT trends and tools in the delivery of education in this pandemic;

Sample Proposal for In-Service Training

- Acquire knowledge on appropriate assessment tools in the new normal;
- Learn test construction applicable in this emergency situations; and
- Learn and employ psychological first aid

V. Proponent: Juan Dela Cruz

VI. Target Clienteles: Elementary Teachers of XYZ district

VII. Schedule of Activities

Activity	Suggested Duration	Indicative Schedule	In-charge
Day 1			
Registration	15 minutes	8:00-8:30	Teacher A
Opening Program	15 minutes	8:30-9:00	Teacher B
How to cope up with challenges in the New Normal of Teaching and Learning	90 minutes	9:00-10:30	Teacher C
ICT trends and tools in the delivery of education in this pandemic	90 minutes	10:30-12:00	Teacher D
Day 2			
Assessment in the New Normal	90 minutes	8:30-10:00	Teacher E
Test Item Analysis	90 minutes	10:00-11:30	Teacher F

Sample Proposal for In-Service Training

Day 3			
Mental Health Awareness and Psychological First Aid	150 minutes	8:30-11:00	Teacher G
Closing Program	30 minutes	11:00-11:30	Teacher H

VIII. Budgetary Requirements
   A. No. of Participants: 50
   B. Budget/participant/Day

Item of Expenditure	Unit Cost	Required No. of Pax	Required No. of Days	Amount
Snacks and Meals	120	15	3	5,400
Token and Certificates of Speaker				1500
Materials				500
				P7,400

IX. Funding Source
   MOOE
   Budget Requirement: P7,400

X. Training Matrix

Date	Topic	Resource Person/Facilitator
Feb. 1, 2021 8:00AM - 12:00AM	How to cope up with challenges in the New Normal of Teaching and Learning	Speaker 1

Sample Proposal for In-Service Training

Date	Topic	Resource Person/Facilitator
	ICT trends and tools in the delivery of education in this pandemic	
Feb. 2, 2021 8:30AM - 11:30AM	Assessment in the New Normal Test Item Analysis	Speaker 2
Feb. 3, 2021 8:30AM - 11:30AM	Mental Health Awareness and Psychological First Aid	Speaker 3

XI. Monitoring and Evaluation Plan

Indicators	Methods	Data Sources	Resources
Learning and Reaction levels of monitoring and evaluation results	Checklist / Survey	Learning Facilitators, Participants, Management	Internet, Phone, laptop, Handouts

XII. Expected Output

(1)   The participants were able to determine ways on how to cope up with challenges in the New Normal of Teaching and Learning. (2) Well-informed participants on the effective usage of ICT trends and tools in the delivery of education in this pandemic. (3) Participants were able to acquire knowledge on appropriate assessment tools in the new normal and learn test construction applicable in this emergency situations. (4) Participants were able to learn and employ psychological first aid in the workplace.

7

MERITORIOUS ACHIEVEMENT

A teacher credited with meritorious achievement such as: *(one involvement will suffice in the awarding of points).*

A teacher must be a trainer or coach of contestants who receives prizes, commendations, or any form of recognition provided they must be FIRST PLACE.

National Winner	**10pts**
Regional Winner	**5pts**
Division Winner	**3pts**
District / Cluster Winner	**1pt**

Athletic coach of athletes or athletic teams who won FIRST PLACE as

National Winner	**10pts**
Regional Winner	**5pts**
Division Winner	**3pts**
District / Cluster Winner	**1pt**

Note*: Points are non-cumulative. The contestant is a bonafide pupil/student of the school. The contest may be academic, socio-cultural, community activity, or athletic competition, not part of a regular lesson/activity. The claim is supported by a certificate of commendation or recognition where the claimant's name as a coach is explicitly stated. Credit points shall be given for each win at any level but not to exceed 10 points. The point for the highest earned place shall be granted if wins are of the same event/activity.*

Coordinator of Boy Scout or Girl Scout Activities (based on DECS Order No. 99, s. 1999)

Documents needed:
1. Official Designation as Coordinator of the activities
2. Approved Proposal of the Scouting Activities
3. Accomplishment Report

BOY SCOUTS
a) Service Awards for Unit Leaders (**Max 1.5 points**)

Bronze	**0.25 pt**
Silver	**0.50 pt**
Gold	**0.75 pt**

b) Merit Award for Unit Leaders **(Max 1.5 points)**

Bronze	**0.25 pt**
Silver	**0.50 pt**
Gold	**0.75 pt**

c) Awards **(Max 2 points)**

Bronze	**0.25 pt**
Silver	**0.75 pt**
Gold	**1.00 pt**

Special Awards such as Plaques/Certificates of Recognition given by the BSP Awards Committee to particular individuals at the council, regional and national levels shall be credited as follows:

Council	**0.50 pt**
Regional	**0.75 pt**
National	**1.25 pts**

GIRL SCOUTS

a. Camp Management Scheme or Trainer's Schemes

AP Training Pool Member	**1.50pts**
GSP Training Pool Member	**1.25pts**
Camper's License or Trainer's Diploma	**1.00pt**
Camper's Permit or Trainer's Credentials	**0.75pt**
Star Holiday Permit / Quarter Master Certificate or specialist Trainers Certificate	**0.50pt**
Campocraft Certificate	**0.25pt**

b. Outstanding Accomplishments

Outstanding Troop Leader	**1.50pts**
Asia Pacific Leader Qualification	**1.25pts**

c. National Awards **(Max 2.0 pts)**
Troop Leaders/Committee members /Other Adults

Gold	**1.25pts**
Silver	**0.75pt**
Bronze	**0.50pt**
Jade, Ruby, and other gems	**0.25pt**

d. Special Awards or Plaques of Recognition given by the Council, National, and Regional Awards Committee shall be awarded as follows:

Council	**0.50pt**
Regional	**0.75pt**
National	**1.25pts**

Notes:

- *Competitions/contests must be those organized/sponsored by the DepEd. For those not organized/sponsored by DepEd, such as those by other government agencies and private organizations, there must be related to education and must have an endorsement by the DepEd.*

- *Winnings for serving as an adviser in group contests in journalism such as Best School Paper are not given points.*

Supporting documents

  (2) Certificate of Recognition as teacher-coach of winning student

  (3) DepEd endorsement (if the competition/contest is not organized/sponsored by the DepEd

8

AUTHORSHIP

Authorship ten (10) points for a book and one (1) point for every article written provided they are scientific and professional articles and the circulation is at least region-wide. Articles in school papers, not included.

Sole Authorship	**10pts**
Co-authorship	**5pts**
Article	**1pt**

Note: *maximum of 10 points only. Song (lyrics & hymn) shall be given one article. Journals or researches that are peer-reviewed international circulation can be awarded 4 points for sole authorship, collaborations divided by the number of collaborators. Thesis and Dissertation in the undergraduate and post studies are not considered.*

Tips on How to Make an Article

Choose a concept

Choose a concept that is new, fascinating, and inside your realm of expertise. Finding a new perspective is also the secret to making the idea stick out for readers. If you introduce new ideas, it means you invite your readers for an engaging intellectual conversation.

Develop Excellent Ideas

It's essential in article writing how to structure your idea so that it conveys your thought. Start with a fantastic twist to inspire the reader to read your article. It might be an issue or a particular case.

Next, clarify the points you're trying to discuss and the facts you're going to use. Please make it clear that your article will be a compelling contribution to the magazine.

Create an outline

Structure and organize the main points into paragraphs so it would be easier for you to write an article.

Edit

Shorten, erase, and revise everything that doesn't add to the context. It's all right to write casually, but don't inject extra words for a valid excuse. Write down the whole paragraph. Set your text aside for a couple of hours or days. Please return to your text again and edit it.

None of us will ever be great authors, and no one wants us to be perfect writers. However, by following these tips and writing naturally, we can improve our performance and sound smarter.

Documents Needed
1. Published book with copyright
2. Original copy of the published article

Other supporting documents:
- *Certification that the candidate wrote the book/article in a certain magazine, date of issue, the page it appeared.*
- *Copy of the Certificate of Copyright Registration*

Sample Outline for an Article Write-up

Introduction
    <u>Thesis Statement</u>

____

    <u>Blueprint showing example</u>

____

Blueprint Example – become the topic sentence of body paragraph 1

    a)   Topic Sentence

____

        i.   Supporting Detail

____

        ii.   Supporting Detail

____

    b)   Concluding Sentence

____

Conclusion
    a. Restate Thesis (including transition)
    b. Summarize Blueprint
    c. General Thought About The Topic (optional)

9

PLUS FACTOR

Awards and commendations of excellence given by authorized DepEd, Division, Regional and National, shall also be given credit. Awards from other agencies, not included.

Division Level	**4pts**
Regional Level	**6pts**
National Level	**10pts**

10

DOCUMENTATION & RANKING

All claims for credits for leadership, potentials, and accomplishments (LPA) should be properly supported by documents. For the purpose of giving points, outputs of the leadership manifested should be presented, as such. As much as possible primary documents such as memoranda, programs, pictures, minutes of the meetings and other documentation will be required.

To determine the rank of the candidates for Master Teacher the credit points earned by each should be added.

Summary

A. Instructional materials/teaching strategies/simplification of work/income-generating project.	20 points
B. Subject Coordinator / Grade Chairman	12 points
C. Chairman of Special Committee	12 points
D. Research	12 points
E. Community Project	12 points
F. In-Service Training	12 points
G. Meritorious Achievement	12 points
H. Authorship	12 points
(Plus Factor)	
Total	100 points

The total shall be arranged from highest to lowest with one having the highest points ranking number 1, the next higher as number 2, etc. In case of a tie, other credits earned outside of the minimum requirements shall be considered but such may not be used again for the next promotion. Actual demonstration and hands-on computer test will be required before appointment. Rank lists are updated every time new vacancies have to be filled up.

BIBLIOGRAPHY

DECS Order No. 57, s. 1997. Further Implementation of the Career Progression System for Master Teachers

DepEd Order No. 16, s. 2017. DepEd Research Management Guidelines

Division Memorandum No. 036, s. 2021. Division Policy Guidelines in the Conduct of Income Generating Project

Division Memorandum No. 169, s. 2020. Guidelines on Writing a Project Proposal for Income Generating Project, Community Service/Outreach and Innovation in Schools

Division Memorandum No. 64, s. 2011. Implementing Rules and Guidelines of the System of Career Progression for Public School Teachers Based on MEC Order No. 10, s. 1979 and Other Issuances

Division Memorandum No. 76, s. 2020. Division Training Proposals and Accomplishment Reports

DO 35, s. 2016. The Learning Action Cell as a K to 12 Basic Education Program School-Based Continuing Professional Development Strategy for the Improvement of Teaching and Learning

MEC Order No. 10, s. 1979. Implementing Rules and Regulations for the System of Career Progression for Public School Teachers

PSB Resolution No. 1, s. 2019. A Resolution Providing for Internal Guidelines on the Hiring, Selection, and Promotion of Teaching, Teaching-Related and Non- Teaching Personnel

Regional Memo No. 185, s. 2020. Harmonized Regional Basic Education Research Agenda

Website

https://www.scribd.com/presentation/407055444/S lac- Workbook-Parts-Specification

About the Author

 **Elmer Z. Ventura** is currently an Elementary School Head Teacher III at DepEd, Schools Division of Tarlac province. He is now finishing his Doctor of Philosophy in Development Education at Tarlac Agricultural University. He holds a Masteral Degree in Educational Leadership at Lyceum-Northwestern University, Bachelor in Elementary Education, CUM LAUDE from Tarlac Agricultural University. He presented his researchers at the regional, national and international levels and published them in professional journals. He is a recipient of Instabright National Awards for Educators, Outstanding Researcher of the Year, Outstanding Writer of the Year, one of the National Outstanding School Heads of LEAD Philippines awards, and *Gawad Ybarra* awardee.

More than being an author, he is cheerful in giving technical assistance to teachers for their career advancements.

www.ingramcontent.com/pod-product-compliance
Lightning Source LLC
LaVergne TN
LVHW050639200726
843506LV00010B/1298